DATE			

COUNTRY VERSE

Lydford Cascade. *From an engraving after T. Allom by W. Taylor*

THE BATSFORD BOOK OF
Country Verse

Edited by Samuel Carr

B. T. BATSFORD LTD · LONDON

First published 1979
Selection © Samuel Carr 1979

ISBN 0 7134 2019 7

Designed by Alan Hamp
Printed and bound in Great Britain
by Butler & Tanner Ltd, Frome and London
for the publishers B. T. Batsford Ltd
4 Fitzhardinge Street, London W1H 0AH

Contents

The Illustrations   6

Introduction   9

Spring   15

Summer   59

Autumn   119

Winter   147

Acknowledgments   187

Index to Authors   189

Index to Artists   190

The Illustrations

Page   **Colour**

45 'In early Spring'. J. W. Inchbold (1830–1913). *The Ashmolean Museum, Oxford*

46 'The Road through the Clover'. Mark Fisher (1841–1923). *The Tate Gallery, London (Photo: John Webb)*

63 Detail from the painting of 'Mr and Mrs Andrews'. Thomas Gainsborough (1727–1788). *Reproduced by courtesy of the Trustees, The National Gallery, London*

64 'The Milkmaid'. Detail of the watercolour by Birket Foster (1825–1899). *The Victoria and Albert Museum, Crown Copyright*

97 'Bellrope Meadow'. From the painting by Stanley Spencer (1891–1959). *The Metropolitan Borough of Rochdale*

98 'The Hayfield'. From the painting by Ford Madox Brown (1821–1893). *The Tate Gallery, London (Photo: John Webb)*

115 'The Isle of Wight'. From the painting by Richard Burchett (1817–1875). *The Victoria and Albert Museum, Crown Copyright*

116 'Near Stoke-by-Nayland'. Detail of the painting by Lionel Constable (1828–1887). *The Tate Gallery, London*

Black and White

Frontispiece: Lydford Cascade. From an illustration by T. Allom, engraved by W. Taylor, in *Devonshire. Illustrated in a Series of Views* (1832)

Page

13 'Middle Hill'. From the painting by George William Mote (1832–1909). *Sotheby Parke Bernet and Co.*

18 'Freshwater in Spring'. From the painting by G. F. Watts (1817–1904). *Private Collection, Rochester, New York; Photograph: The Fine Art Society Ltd., London*

21 'Cascade at Ambleside'. From the watercolour by Francis Towne (1808–1877). *The Ashmolean Museum, Oxford*

24 & 25 'Golding Constable's Flower Garden'. From the painting by John Constable (1776–1837). *Ipswich Museum Committee*

28 'Hatfield'. From an etching by John Middleton (1827–1856). *William Weston Gallery, London*

33 'Luccombe Chine, Isle of Wight'. From the watercolour by H. A. Bowler (1824–1903). *Victoria and Albert Museum, Crown Copyright*

37 'Rosemary, Devon'. From the lithograph by Robert Bevan (1865–1925). *William Weston Gallery*

40 & 41 'Wide Pastures, Sussex'. From the watercolour by Thomas Collier (1840–1891). *Victoria and Albert Museum, Crown Copyright*

43 'At Scoutton'. From the etching by John Crome (1768–1821). *William Weston Gallery*

51 'Buttermere Lake'. From the painting by J. M. W. Turner (1775–1851). *The Tate Gallery, London*

66 & 67 'Sweet Summer Time'. From the painting by Richard Redgrave (1804–1888). *Victoria and Albert Museum, Crown Copyright*

68 'Cray Fields'. From the etching by Graham Sutherland (1903–). *The British Museum* © A.D.A.G.P. Paris, 1978

72 'The Tree Trunk'. From a pen and ink drawing by Harold Gilman (1876–1919). *Private Collection*

77 'Study of Trees'. From the watercolour by John Crome. *Victoria and Albert Museum, Crown Copyright*

85 Kentish Landscape near Winchelsea: detail from 'The Blind Girl'. From the painting by J. E. Millais (1829–1896). *By permission of Birmingham Museums and Art Gallery*

88 & 89 'Cornard Wood'. From the painting by Thomas Gainsborough (1727–1788). *Reproduced by courtesy of the Trustees, The National Gallery, London*

93 'The Skylark'. From the etching by Samuel Palmer (1805–1881). *William Weston Gallery*

101 'Summer Evening'. From the mezzotint by David Lucas (1802–1881) after John Constable (1776–1837). *William Weston Gallery*

105 'Panshanger Park'. From the painting by Spencer Gore (1878–1914). *Royal Albert Memorial Museum, Exeter*

108 'Great Rydal Lake'. Engraved by Edward Finden (1792–1857) after William Westall (1781–1850). From an illustration to *Great Britain Illustrated* (1830)

113 'The Sleeping Shepherd'. From an etching by Samuel Palmer (1805–1881). *William Weston Gallery*

125 'Postwick Grove'. From an etching by Miles Edmund Cotman (1811–1858). *William Weston Gallery*

130 & 131 'Reapers: Noonday Rest'. From the painting by John Linnell (1792–1882). *The Tate Gallery, London*

135 'Kerswell, Devon'. From the watercolour by John White Abbott (1763–1851). *The Victoria and Albert Museum, Crown Copyright*

137 'Folding the last Sheep'. From the etching by Samuel Palmer (1805–1881). *Colnaghi and Co. Ltd.*

139 'The Cornfield Shelter'. From the painting by John Linnell (1792–1882). *Tunbridge Wells Art Gallery*

143 'Herefordshire and the Malvern Hills: Harvest Scene'. From the painting by G. R. Lewis (1782–1871). *The Tate Gallery, London*

144 'Stray Rabbits'. Detail of a painting by Robert Collinson (1832–1890). *The Victoria and Albert Museum, Crown Copyright*

150 'The Teme at Downton'. From the watercolour by Thomas Hearne (1744–1877). *The Victoria and Albert Museum, Crown Copyright*

156 & 157 'Opening the Fold'. From the etching by Samuel Palmer (1805–1881). *Colnaghi and Co. Ltd.*

168 & 169 'Lower Norwood'. From the painting by Camille Pissarro (1830–1903). *By courtesy of the Trustees, The National Gallery, London*

173 'Avenue of Oaks'. From a steel engraving by James D. Cooper after W. H. J. Boot. Reproduced from Mary Russell Mitford, *Our Village* (1879 edition)

176 'The Thames near Marble Hill'. From the painting by Richard Wilson (1714–1782). *The Tate Gallery, London*

178 'Driving Sheep'. From the etching by James Stark (1794–1859). *William Weston Gallery*

181 'Beech Trees'. From the painting by Alfred Priest (1810–1850). *Norfolk Museums Service (Castle Museum, Norwich)*

185 'The Deep Lane'. From a steel engraving after W. H. J. Boot by James D. Cooper. From Mary Russell Mitford, *Our Village* (1879)

186 'A Field of Green Corn'. From the painting by William Davis (1812–1873). *Private Collection*

The front endpaper is reproduced from the painting, 'A Ploughed Field', by J. S. Cotman (1782–1842). (*Leeds Art Gallery*.) The back endpaper is from 'A Cornfield', by Peter De Wint (1784–1849). (*The Victoria and Albert Museum*.) The decorations on the half-title pages to the sections and elsewhere are from woodcuts by Thomas Bewick (1753–1828).

Introduction

Any selection of poetry reflects the personal taste of its editor. The bias in this anthology is towards the specific and the topographical and away from the subjective and the pantheistic. The poems which have been chosen are, in other words, generally about a particular place at a particular time of day. The scene is not used as a pretext from which to draw a moral on, as it might be, the transience of human life, but is described for its own sake. (With, it must be admitted, one or two exceptions, among them W. R. Rodgers' feeling poem 'The Harvest Field'.)

All editors of anthologies like to surprise the reader with verse which they hope is unfamiliar. The danger lies in going to the opposite extreme and excluding great poems on account of their familiarity. It is as well to remember that the classics *are* the classics because they are the best, just as the poetry that is best known is on the whole the poetry that is best worth knowing. So, in whole or in part, Goldsmith's 'Deserted Village' will here be found, and so will 'L'Allegro', Gray's 'Elegy', Cowper's 'Poplar Field' and Hardy's 'Weathers'. But there are also many other poems which are worth including even if their authors — Henry Ellison, William Browne, Richard Watson Dixon, Bernard Barton, for example — are now little known.

The pictures are intended to complement the poems rather than to illustrate them. Sometimes the echo is as close a one as a shared title: Wordsworth's and Samuel Palmer's 'Skylark', and the verses by John Clare and the Constable-Lucas mezzotint 'Summer Evening' are cases in point. More commonly the reproductions form a parallel anthology to the poems. For the poets as for the painters the English countryside was a discovery largely of the nineteenth century. Up to then, while Cowper may have written about particular scenes just as Gainsborough had occasionally painted them, the usual approach had been a generalised one. It is true that Samuel Johnson (himself no country lover) believed otherwise. In his life of Sir John Denham (1616–1669) Dr Johnson claimed that 'Cooper's Hill' 'is the work that confers upon him [Denham] the rank and dignity of an original author. He seems to have been, at least among us, the author of a species of local composition that may be denominated *local poetry*, of which the fundamental subject is some particular landscape, to be poetically described. . . .' Yet to our eyes the picture called up by 'Cooper's Hill' is, in spite of its title, little less formalised than an Elizabethan pastoral.

In any event the selection both of poems and of pictures has been drawn principally from the period after 1800. There are exceptions, but the poets and the painters were as often as not townsmen. A Wordsworth or a Clare, a Constable or a Gainsborough might spontaneously relish the countryside. More commonly it needed the urban horrors that too often came with the Industrial Revolution to suggest to town-dwellers that there existed a rural Paradise Lost from which they had been banished but which they might one day hope to regain. It may also be the case that, as cities and towns became the customary places in which to live, poets grew reconciled to urban living. Whatever the reason, Hardy was the last great poet to take the country and its activities as a principal theme.

The arrangement which has been followed with the poems in this book is roughly a seasonal one, interspersed by verses which belong to no evident time of the year. The alternatives were: according to date, but in that case the selection would have appeared capricious and unrepresentative; or according to place, but then whole stretches of country — Yorkshire, for instance — would have been seen to be omitted while others, like the Lakes, would have been over-favoured. So the present loosely seasonal arrangement has been imposed, arbitrary as it too often is.

The pleasure of editing an anthology such as this is one of recollection and rediscovery: old friends met again and new ones established. The editor hopes that he may have succeeded in sharing some of that enjoyment.

It is perhaps worth adding, by way of conclusion, that to read poetry *in extenso* is almost always uphill work. Like some other refined pleasures, that in poetry is best savoured in snatches.

Such, it is suggested, is the best way to approach this collection: it should be taken up, read at random, put down, and later, it is hoped, returned to again.

A country life

from: to John Driden of Chesterton

How blessed is he, who leads a country life,
Unvex'd with anxious cares and void of strife!
Who studying peace, and shunning civil rage,
Enjoy'd his youth, and now enjoys his age:
All who deserve his love, he makes his own;
And, to be lov'd himself, needs only to be known.

JOHN DRYDEN (1637–1700)

13

SPRING

from: *The Song of Solomon*

My beloved spake, and said unto me, Rise up, my love, my fair one, and come away.

For, lo, the winter is past, the rain is over and gone;

The flowers appear on the earth; the time of the singing of birds is come, and the voice of the turtle is heard in our land;

The fig tree putteth forth her green figs, and the vines with the tender grape give a good smell. Arise, my love, my fair one, and come away.

Written in March

While resting on the bridge at the foot of Brother's Water

The Cock is crowing,
The stream is flowing,
The small birds twitter,
The lake doth glitter,
The green field sleeps in the sun;
The oldest and youngest
Are at work with the strongest;
The cattle are grazing,
Their heads never raising;
There are forty feeding like one!

Like an army defeated
The snow hath retreated,
And now doth fare ill
On the top of the bare hill;
The ploughboy is whooping — anon — anon:
There's joy in the mountains;
There's life in the fountains;
Small clouds are sailing,
Blue sky prevailing;
The rain is over and gone!

WILLIAM WORDSWORTH (1770–1850)

17

Freshwater in Spring. *G. F. Watts*

A backward Spring

The trees are afraid to put forth buds,
And there is timidity in the grass;
The plots lie gray where gouged by spuds,
     And whether next week will pass
Free of sly sour winds is the fret of each bush
     Of barberry waiting to bloom.

Yet the snowdrop's face betrays no gloom,
And the primrose pants in its heedless push,
Though the myrtle asks if it's worth the fight
     This year with frost and rime
     To venture one more time
On delicate leaves and buttons of white
From the selfsame bough as at last year's prime,
And never to ruminate on or remember
What happened to it in mid-December.

THOMAS HARDY (1840–1928)

After the storm

After the rain had ceased
We wandered out again.
The trees and ripening grain
With beauty were increased;
And the flowers, heavy and bent,
Dropped an immortal scent.

There was no sunshine yet
As we strolled along the lane,
Slow, with a sweet regret
That still must cherish pain
Of angry word and look.
The boughs of love still shook
Keen drops about us there,
As closer still than ever,
We breathed the silver air,
Chill aftermath, but pure,
A passion to endure,
A love no storm could sever.

RICHARD CHURCH (1893–1972)

The waterfall

from: The Seasons

Smooth to the shelving brink a copious flood
Rolls fair, and placid; where collected all,
In one impetuous torrent, down the steep
It thundering shoots, and shakes the country round.
At first, an azure sheet, it rushes broad;
Then whitening by degrees, as prone it falls,
And from the loud-resounding rocks below
Dash'd in a cloud of foam, it sends aloft
A hoary mist, and forms a ceaseless shower.
Nor can the tortur'd wave here find repose;
But, raging still amid the shaggy rocks,
Now flashes o'er the scatter'd fragments, now
Aslant the hollowed channel rapid darts;
And falling fast from gradual slope to slope,
With wild infracted course, and lessened roar,
It gains a safer bed; and steals, at last,
Along the mazes of the quiet vale.

JAMES THOMSON (1700–1748)

Cascade at Ambleside. *Francis Towne*
(Ashmolean Museum, Oxford)

Sonnet

After dark vapors have oppress'd our plains
    For a long dreary season, comes a day
    Born of the gentle South, and clears away
From the sick heavens all unseemly stains.
The anxious month, relieved of its pains,
    Takes as a long-lost right the feel of May;
    The eyelids with the passing coolness play
Like rose leaves with the drip of Summer rains.
The calmest thoughts come round us; as of leaves
    Budding — fruit ripening in stillness — Autumn suns
Smiling at eve upon the quiet sheaves —
Sweet Sappho's cheek — a smiling infant's breath —
    The gradual sand that through an hour-glass runs —
A woodland rivulet — a Poet's death.

JOHN KEATS (1792–1821)

Pleasure it is

Pleasure it is
To hear, iwis,
The birdës sing.
The deer in the dale,
The sheep in the vale,
The corn springing;
God's purveyance
For sustenance
It is for man.
Then we always
To him give praise,
And thank him than,
And thank him than.

WILLIAM CORNISH (D. 1523?)

Thaw

Over the land freckled with snow half-thawed
The speculating rooks at their nests cawed
And saw from elm-tops, delicate as flower of grass,
What we below could not see, Winter pass.

EDWARD THOMAS (1878–1917)

Golding Constable's Garden. *John Constable*

Afton Water

Flow gently, sweet Afton, among thy green braes,
Flow gently, I'll sing thee a song in thy praise;
My Mary's asleep by thy murmuring stream,
Flow gently, sweet Afton, disturb not her dream.

Thou stock-dove whose echo resounds thro' the glen,
Ye wild whistling blackbirds in yon thorny den,
Thou green-crested lapwing, thy screaming forbear,
I charge you disturb not my slumbering fair.

How lofty, sweet Afton, thy neighbouring hills,
Far mark'd with the courses of clear winding rills;
There daily I wander as noon rises high,
My flocks and my Mary's sweet cot in my eye.

How pleasant thy banks and green valleys below,
Where wild in the woodlands the primroses blow;
There oft as mild ev'ning weeps over the lea,
The sweet-scented birk shades my Mary and me.

Thy crystal stream, Afton, how lovely it glides,
And winds by the cot where my Mary resides;
How wanton thy waters her snowy feet lave,
As gathering sweet flow'rets she stems thy clear wave.

Flow gently, sweet Afton, among thy green braes,
Flow gently, sweet river, the theme of my lays;
My Mary's asleep by thy murmuring stream,
Flow gently, sweet Afton, disturb not her dream.

ROBERT BURNS (1759–1796)

Stay, Spring

Stay, spring, for by this ruthless haste
You turn all good to waste;
Look, how the blackthorn now
Changes to trifling dust upon the bough.

Where blossom from the wild pear shakes
Too rare a china breaks,
And though the cuckoos shout
They will forget their name ere June is out.

That thrush too, that with beadlike eye
Watches each passer-by,
Is warming at her breast
A brood that when they fly rob their own nest.

So late begun, so early ended!
Lest I should be offended
Take warning, spring, and stay
Or I might never turn to look your way.

ANDREW YOUNG (1885–1971)

The woods and banks

The woods and banks of England now,
  Late coppered with dead leaves and old,
Have made the early violets grow,
  And bulge with knots of primrose gold.
Hear how the blackbird flutes away,
  Whose music scorns to sleep at night:
Hear how the cuckoo shouts all day
  For echoes — to the world's delight:
Hallo, you imp of wonder, you —
Where are you now, cuckoo? Cuckoo!

W. H. DAVIES (1871–1940)

from:

The Oak-Tree

The girt woak tree that's in the dell!
Ther's noo tree I da love so well;
Var in thik tree, when I wer young,
I of'en climb'd an' of'en zwung,
An' pick'd the green-rin'd yacors, shed
In wrestlèn storm-winds vrom his head.
An' down below's the cloty brook
Wher I did vish wi' line an' hook,
An' beät, in plâysome dips an' zwims,
The foamy stream wi' white-skinn'd lims.
An' there my mother nimbly shot
Her knittèn-needles, as she zot
At evemen down below the wide
Woak's head, wi' fäther at her zide.
An' I've a plây'd wi' many a buoy,
That's now a man an' gone awoy;
  Zoo I da like noo tree so well
  'S the girt woak tree that's in the dell.

WILLIAM BARNES (1801–1886)

Hatfield. *John Middleton*

Early Spring

from: The First of April

Scant along the ridgy land
The beans their new-born ranks expand:
The fresh-turned soil with tender blades
Thinly the sprouting barley shades:
Fringing the forest's devious edge,
Half robed appears the hawthorn hedge;
Or to the distant eye displays
Weakly green its budding sprays.

The swallow, for a moment seen,
Skims in haste the village green:
From the gray moor, on feeble wing,
The screaming plovers idly spring:
The butterfly, gay-painted soon,
Explores awhile the tepid noon;
And fondly trusts its tender dyes
To fickle suns, and flattering skies.

Fraught with a transient, frozen shower,
If a cloud should haply lower,
Sailing o'er the landscape dark,
Mute on a sudden is the lark;
But when gleams the sun again
O'er the pearl-besprinkled plain,
And from behind his watery veil
Looks through the thin descending hail;
She mounts, and, lessening to the sight,
Salutes the blithe return of light,
And high her tuneful track pursues
Mid the dim rainbow's scattered hues.

Where in venerable rows
Widely waving oaks inclose
The moat of yonder antique hall,
Swarm the rooks with clamorous call;
And to the toils of nature true,
Wreath their capacious nests anew.

THOMAS WARTON (1728–1790)

Spring pools

These pools that, though in forests, still reflect
The total sky almost without defect,
And like the flowers beside them, chill and shiver,
Will like the flowers beside them soon be gone,
And yet not out by any brook or river,
But up by roots to bring dark foliage on.

The trees that have it in their pent-up buds
To darken nature and be summer woods—
Let them think twice before they use their powers
To blot out and drink up and sweep away
These flowery waters and these watery flowers
From snow that melted only yesterday.

ROBERT FROST (1875–1963)

April

from: In Memoriam

Now fades the last long streak of snow,
  Now burgeons every maze of quick
  About the flowering squares, and thick
By ashen roots the violets blow.

Now rings the woodland loud and long,
  The distance takes a lovelier hue,
  And drown'd in yonder living blue,
The lark becomes a sightless song.

Now dance the lights on lawn and lea,
  The flocks are whiter down the vale,
  And milkier every milky sail
On winding stream or distant sea;

Where now the seamew pipes, or dives
  In yonder greening gleam, and fly
  The happy birds, that change their sky
To build and brood; that live their lives

From land to land; and in my breast
  Spring wakens too; and my regret
  Becomes an April violet,
And buds and blossoms like the rest.

ALFRED, LORD TENNYSON (1809–1892)

Luccombe Chine. *H. A. Bowler*

The rain

I hear leaves drinking rain;
   I hear rich leaves on top
Giving the poor beneath
   Drop after drop;
'Tis a sweet noise to hear
These green leaves drinking near.

And when the Sun comes out,
   After this rain shall stop,
A wondrous light will fill
   Each dark, round drop;
I hope the Sun shines bright;
'Twill be a lovely sight.

W. H. DAVIES (1871–1940)

Spring

from: Windsor-Forest

In genial spring, beneath the quiv'ring shade,
Where cooling vapours breathe along the mead,
The patient fisher takes his silent stand,
Intent, his angle trembling in his hand:
With looks unmov'd, he hopes the scaly breed,
And eyes the dancing cork, and bending reed.
Our plenteous streams a various race supply,
The bright-ey'd perch with fins of Tyrian dye,
The silver eel, in shining volumes roll'd,
The yellow carp, in scales bedrop'd with gold,
Swift trouts, diversify'd with crimson stains,
And pykes, the tyrants of the watry plains.

ALEXANDER POPE (1688–1744)

34

March morning unlike others

Blue haze. Bees hanging in air at the hive-mouth.
Crawling in prone stupor of sun
On the hive-lip. Snowdrops. Two buzzards,
Still-wings, each
Magnetised to the other
Float orbits.
Cattle standing warm. Lit, happy stillness.
A raven, under the hill,
Coughing among bare oaks.
Aircraft, elated, splitting blue.
Leisure to stand. The knee-deep mud at the trough
Stiffening. Lambs freed to be foolish.

The earth invalid, dropsied, bruised, wheeled
Out into the sun,
After the frightful operation.
She lies back, wounds undressed to the sun,
To be healed,
Sheltered from the sneapy chill creeping North wind,
Leans back, eyes closed, exhausted, smiling
Into the sun. Perhaps dozing a little.
While we sit, and smile, and wait, and know
She is not going to die.

TED HUGHES (1930–)

Dartmoor

I crossed the furze-grown table-land
   And neared the northern vales,
That lay perspicuously planned
   In lesser hills and dales.
Then, rearward, in a slow review,
   Fell Dartmoor's jagged lines;
Around were dross-heaps, red and blue,
   Old shafts of gutted mines,
Impetuous currents copper-stained,
   Wheels steam-urged with a roar,
Sluice-guiding grooves, strong works that strained
   With freight of upheaved ore.
And then, the train, with shock on shock,
   Swift rush and birth-scream dire,
Grew from the bosom of the rock,
   And passed in noise and fire.
With brazen throb, with vital stroke,
   It went, far heard, far seen,
Setting a track of shining smoke
   Upon the pastoral green.
Then, bright drops, lodged in budding trees,
   Were loosed in sudden showers,
Touched by the novel western breeze,
   Friend of the backward flowers.
Then rose the Church of Tavistock,
   The rain still falling there;
But sunny Dartmoor seemed to mock
   The gloom with cheerful glare.
About the West the gilt vane reeled
   And poised; and with sweet art,
The sudden, jangling changes pealed
   Until, around my heart,

Rosemary, Devon. *Robert Bevan*

Conceits of brighter times, of times
    The brighter for past storms,
Clung thick as bees, when brazen chimes
    Call down the hiveless swarms.

COVENTRY PATMORE (1823–1896)

37

April

Oh, to be in England now that April's there,
And whoever wakes in England sees, some morning,
   unaware,
That the lowest boughs and the brushwood sheaf
Round the elm-tree bole are in tiny leaf,
While the chaffinch sings on the orchard bough
    In England — now!

   And, after April, when May follows,
And the whitethroat builds, and all the swallows!
Hark, where my blossomed pear-tree in the hedge
   Leans to the field and scatters on the clover
Blossoms and dewdrops — at the bent spray's edge —
   That's the wise thrush; he sings each song twice over,
Lest you should think he never could recapture
    The first fine careless rapture!
And though the fields look rough with hoary dew,
All will be gay when noontide wakes anew
The buttercups, the little children's dower
—Far brighter than this gaudy melon-flower!

ROBERT BROWNING (1812–1889)

Up on the downs

Up on the downs the red-eyed kestrels hover,
Eyeing the grass.
The field-mouse flits like a shadow into the cover
As their shadows pass.

Men are burning the gorse on the down's shoulder;
A drift of smoke
Glitters with fire and hangs, and the skies smoulder,
And the lungs choke.

Once the tribe did thus on the downs, on these down burning
Men in the frame,
Crying to the gods of the downs till their brains were turning
And the gods came.

And to-day on the downs, in the wind, the hawks, the grasses,
In blood and air,
Something passes me and cries as it passes,
On the chalk downland bare.

JOHN MASEFIELD (1878–1967)

Wide Pastures, Sussex. *Thomas Collier*

The Spring

Now that the Winter's gone, the earth hath lost
Her snow-white robes; and now no more the frost
Candies the grass, or casts an icy cream
Upon the silver lake or crystal stream:
But the warm sun thaws the benumbed earth,
And makes it tender; gives a sacred birth
To the dead swallow; wakes in hollow tree
The drowsy cuckoo and the humble-bee.
Now do a choir of chirping minstrels bring
In triumph to the world the youthful Spring:
The valleys, hills, and woods in rich array
Welcome the coming of the long'd-for May
Now all things smile: only my love doth lour,
Nor hath the scalding noonday sun the power
To melt that marble ice which still doth hold
Her heart congeal'd, and makes her pity cold.
The ox, which lately did for shelter fly
Into the stall, doth now securely lie
In open fields; and love no more is made
By the fireside, but in the cooler shade
Amyntas now doth with his Chloris sleep
Under a sycamore, and all things keep
    Time with the season: only she doth carry
    June in her eyes, in her heart January.

THOMAS CAREW (1598–1639)

The trees

The trees are coming into leaf
Like something almost being said;
The recent buds relax and spread,
Their greenness is a kind of grief.

Is it that they are born again
And we grow old? No, they die too.
Their yearly trick of looking new
Is written down in rings of grain.

Yet still the unresting castles thresh
In fullgrown thickness every May.
Last year is dead, they seem to say,
Begin afresh, afresh, afresh.

PHILIP LARKIN (1922–   )

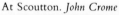
At Scoutton. *John Crome*

The first Spring day

I wonder if the sap is stirring yet,
If wintry birds are dreaming of a mate,
If frozen snowdrops feel as yet the sun
And crocus fires are kindling one by one:
    Sing, robin, sing;
I still am sore in doubt concerning Spring.

I wonder if the springtide of this year
Will bring another Spring both lost and dear;
If heart and spirit will find out their Spring,
Or if the world alone will bud and sing:
    Sing, hope, to me;
Sweet notes, my hope, soft notes for memory.

The sap will surely quicken soon or late,
The tardiest bird will twitter to a mate;
So Spring must dawn again with warmth and bloom,
Or in this world, or in the world to come:
    Sing, voice of Spring,
Till I too blossom and rejoice and sing.

CHRISTINA ROSSETTI (1830–1894)

In early Spring. *J. W. Inchbold*
(The Ashmolean Museum, Oxford)

Spring flowers

from: The Seasons

Along the blushing Borders, bright with Dew,
And in yon mingled Wilderness of Flowers,
Fair-handed Spring unbosoms every Grace:
Throws out the Snow-drop, and the Crocus first;
The Daisy, Primrose, Violet darkly blue,
And Polyanthus of unnumber'd Dyes;
The yellow Wall-Flower, stain'd with iron Brown;
And lavish Stock that scents the Garden round:
From the soft Wing of vernal Breezes shed,
Anemonies; Auriculas, enrich'd
With shining Meal o'er all their velvet Leaves;
And full Renunculas, of glowing Red.
Then comes the Tulip-Race, where Beauty plays
Her idle Freaks: from Family diffus'd
To Family, as flies the Father-Dust,
The varied Colours run; and while they *break*
On the charm'd Eye, th' exulting Florist marks,
With secret Pride, the Wonders of his Hand.
No gradual Bloom is wanting; from the Bud,
First-born of Spring, to Summer's musky Tribes:
Nor Hyacinths, deep-purpled; nor Jonquils,
Of potent Fragrance; nor Narcissus fair,
As o'er the fabled Fountain hanging still;
Nor broad Carnations; nor gay-spotted Pinks;
Nor, shower'd from every Bush, the Damask-rose:
Infinite Numbers, Delicacies, Smells,
With Hues on Hues Expression cannot paint,
The Breath of Nature, and her endless Bloom.

JAMES THOMSON (1700–1748)

Road through the Clover. *Mark Fisher*

The progress of Spring

The groundflame of the crocus breaks the mould,
  Fair Spring slides hither o'er the Southern sea,
Wavers on her thin stem the snowdrop cold
  That trembles not to kisses of the bee:
Come, Spring, for now from all the dripping eaves
  The spear of ice has wept itself away,
And hour by hour unfolding woodbine leaves
  O'er his uncertain shadow droops the day.
She comes! The loosen'd rivulets run;
  The frost-bead melts upon her golden hair;
Her mantle, slowly greening in the Sun,
  Now wraps her close, now arching leaves her bare
  To breaths of balmier air;

Up leaps the lark, gone wild to welcome her,
  About her glance the tits, and shriek the jays,
Before her skims the jubilant woodpecker,
  The linnet's bosom blushes at her gaze,
While round her brows a woodland culver flits,
  Watching her large light eyes and gracious looks,
And in her open palm a halcyon sits
  Patient — the secret splendour of the brooks.
Come, Spring! She comes on waste and wood,
  On farm and field: but enter also here,
Diffuse thyself at will thro' all my blood,
  And, tho' thy violet sicken into sere,
  Lodge with me all the year!

Once more a downy drift against the brakes,
  Self-darken'd in the sky, descending slow!
But gladly see I thro' the wavering flakes
  Yon blanching apricot like snow in snow.
These will thine eyes not brook in forest-paths,
  On their perpetual pine, nor round the beech;

They fuse themselves to little spicy baths,
   Solved in the tender blushes of the peach;
They lose themselves and die
   On that new life that gems the hawthorn line;
Thy gay lent-lilies wave and put them by,
   And out once more in varnish'd glory shine
   Thy stars of celandine.

ALFRED, LORD TENNYSON (1809–1892)

from:

The shadowy waters

I walked among the seven woods of Coole,
Shan-walla, where a willow-bordered pond
Gathers the wild duck from the winter dawn;
Shady Kyle-dortha; sunnier Kyle-na-no,
Where many hundred squirrels are as happy
As though they had been hidden by green boughs
Where old age cannot find them; Pairc-na-lee,
Where hazel and ash and privet blind the paths;
Dim Pairc-na-carraig, where the wild bees fling
Their sudden fragrances on the green air;
Dim Pairc-na-tarav, where enchanted eyes
Have seen immortal, mild, proud shadows walk;
Dim Inchy wood, that hides badger and fox
And marten-cat, and borders that old wood
Wise Biddy Early called the wicked wood;
Seven odours, seven murmurs, seven woods.

W. B. YEATS (1865–1939)

By the calm lake

from: An Evening Walk

Sweet are the sounds that mingle from afar,
Heard by calm lakes, as peeps the folding star,
Where the duck dabbles 'mid the rustling sedge,
And feeding pike starts from the water's edge,
Or the swan stirs the reeds, his neck and bill
Wetting, that drip upon the water still;
And heron, as resounds the trodden shore,
Shoots upward, darting his long neck before.
While, by the scene compos'd the breast subsides,
Nought wakens or disturbs its tranquil tides;
Nought but the char that for the may-fly leaps,
And breaks the mirror of the circling deeps;
Or clock, that blind against the wanderer born,
Drops at his feet, and stills his droning horn.
— The whistling swain that plods his ringing way
Where the slow waggon winds along the bay;
The sugh of swallow flocks that twittering sweep,
The solemn curfew swinging long and deep;
The talking boat that moves with pensive sound,
Or drops his anchor down with plunge profound;
Of boys that bathe remote the faint uproar,
And restless piper wearying out the shore;
These all to swell the village murmurs blend,
That soften'd from the water-head descend.

WILLIAM WORDSWORTH (1770–1850)

Buttermere. *J. M. W. Turner*

Essex

'The vagrant visitor erstwhile,'
  My colour-plate book says to me,
'Could wend by hedgerow-side and stile,
  From Benfleet down to Leigh-on-Sea.'

And as I turn the colour-plates
  Edwardian Essex opens wide,
Mirrored in ponds and seen through gates,
  Sweet uneventful countryside.

Like streams the little by-roads run
  Through oats and barley round a hill
To where blue willows catch the sun
  By some white weather-boarded mill.

'A summer Idyll Matching Tye'
  'At Havering-atte-Bower, the Stocks'
And cobbled pathways lead the eye
  To cottage doors and hollyhocks.

Far Essex, — fifty miles away
  The level wastes of sucking mud
Where distant barges high with hay
  Come sailing in upon the flood.

Near Essex of the River Lea
   And anglers out with hook and worm
And Epping Forest glades where we
   Had beanfeasts with my father's firm.

At huge and convoluted pubs
   They used to set us down from brakes
In that half-land of football clubs
   Which London near the Forest makes.

The deepest Essex few explore
   Where steepest thatch is sunk in flowers
And out of elm and sycamore
   Rise flinty fifteenth-century towers.

I see the little branch line go
   By white farms roofed in red and brown,
The old Great Eastern winding slow
   To some forgotten country town.

Now yarrow chokes the railway track,
   Brambles obliterate the stile,
No motor coach can take me back
   To that Edwardian 'erstwhile'.

JOHN BETJEMAN (1906–)

Northumberland landscape

from: The Pleasures of Imagination

                                        O ye dales
Of Tyne, and ye most ancient woodlands; where,
Oft as the giant flood obliquely strides,
And his banks open, and his lawns extend,
Stops short the pleased traveller to view,
Presiding o'er the scene, some rustic tower
Founded by Norman or by Saxon hands:
O ye Northumbrian shades, which overlook
The rocky pavement and the mossy falls
Of solitary Wensbeck's limpid stream;
How gladly I recall your well-known seats,
Beloved of old, and that delightful time
When, all alone, for many a summer's day,
I wandered through your calm recesses, led
In silence by some powerful hand unseen.

MARK AKENSIDE (1721–1770)

Birds in Spring

from: The Seasons

The Black-bird whistles from the thorny Brake;
The mellow Bullfinch answers from the Grove:
Nor are the Linnets, o'er the flowering Furze
Pour'd out profusely, silent. Join'd to These
Innumerous Songsters, in the freshening Shade
Of new-sprung Leaves, their Modulations mix
Mellifluous. The Jay, the Rook, the Daw,
And each harsh Pipe discordant heard alone,
Aid the full Concert: while the Stock-dove breathes
A melancholy Murmur thro' the whole.

JAMES THOMSON (1700–1748)

Spring

from: *The Psalms of David*

Now the winds are all composure,
   But the breath upon the bloom,
Blowing sweet o'er each inclosure
   Grateful off'rings of perfume.

Tansy, calaminth and daisies
   On the river's margin thrive;
And accompany the mazes
   Of the stream that leaps alive.

Muse, accordant to the season,
   Give the numbers life and air;
When the sounds and objects reason
   In behalf of praise and pray'r.

All the scenes of nature quicken,
   By the genial spirit fann'd;
And the painted beauties thicken,
   Colour'd by the master's hand.

Earth her vigour repossessing
   As the blasts are held in ward,
Blessing heap'd and press'd on blessing,
   Yield the measure of the Lord.

Beeches, without order seemly,
   Shade the flow'rs of annual birth,
And the lily smiles supremely,
   Mention'd by the Lord on earth.

Couslips seize upon the fallow,
  And the cardamine in white,
Where the corn-flow'rs join the mallow,
  Joy and health, and thrift unite.

Study sits beneath her arbour,
  By the bason's glossy side;
While the boat from out its harbour
  Exercise and pleasure guide.

Pray'r and praise be mine employment,
  Without grudging or regret;
Lasting life, and long enjoyment
  Are not here, and are not yet.

Hark! aloud, the black-bird whistles,
  With surrounding fragrance blest,
And the goldfinch in the thistles
  Makes provision for her nest.

Ev'n the hornet hives his honey,
  Bluecap builds his stately dome,
And the rocks supply the coney
  With a fortress and an home.

CHRISTOPHER SMART (1722–1771)

Spider's web

The fairest Home I ever knew
Was founded in an Hour
By Parties also that I knew
A spider and a Flower —
A manse of mechlin and of Floss —

EMILY DICKINSON (1830–1886)

SUMMER

On May *Morning*

Now the bright morning star, Dayes harbinger,
Comes dancing from the East, and leads with her
The Flowry *May*, who from her green lap throws
The yellow Cowslip, and the pale Primrose.
   Hail bounteous *May* that dost inspire
   Mirth and youth and warm desire,
   Woods and Groves are of thy dressing,
   Hill and Dale doth boast thy blessing.
Thus we salute thee with our early Song,
And welcom thee, and wish thee long.

JOHN MILTON (1608–1674)

Cornfields

Corn waves in the wind:
A sigh, early and late.
The eye of the barley is blind
When the stalk is stiff and straight.

Ears, ripening, rise,
Then gold, heavily fall;
The breath of nativity sighs:
The star is laid in the stall.

Learn, learn of the corn
Of things coming to pass,
Of wings, and a foal unborn
To the mare asleep in the grass.

Crest follows on crest;
A sigh moving in air,
A rustling of wings in the nest
Ascends from the dreaming mare.

Birth's tremor within
The fruit earth has concealed,
Does it summon life to begin
And the sun to reap the field,

Joy weighing at dusk
The scales, heavy and light,
The balance of ear and husk
Daybreak dreaming of night?

VERNON WATKINS (1906–   )

Suffolk Landscape. *Thomas Gainsborough*

Country delights

from: L'Allegro

To hear the Lark begin his flight,
And singing startle the dull night,
From his watch-towre in the skies,
Till the dappled dawn doth rise;
Then to com in spight of sorrow,
And at my window bid good morrow,
Through the Sweet-Briar, or the Vine,
Or the twisted Eglantine.
While the Cock with lively din,
Scatters the rear of darknes thin,
And to the stack, or the Barn dore,
Stoutly struts his Dames before,
Oft list'ning how the Hounds and horn,
Clearly rouse the slumbring morn,
From the side of som Hoar Hill,
Through the high wood echoing shrill.
Som time walking not unseen
By Hedge-row Elms, on Hillocks green,
Right against the Eastern gate,
Where the great Sun begins his state,
Rob'd in flames, and Amber light,
The clouds in thousand Liveries dight,
While the Plowman neer at hand,
Whistles ore the Furrow'd Land,
And the Milkmaid singeth blithe,
And the Mower whets his sithe,
And every Shepherd tells his tale
Under the Hawthorn in the dale.
Streit mine eye hath caught new pleasures
Whilst the Lantskip round it measures,
Russet Lawns, and Fallows Gray,
Where the nibling flocks do stray,
Mountains on whose barren brest
The labouring clouds do often rest:
Meadows trim with Daisies pide,
Shallow Brooks, and Rivers wide.

The Milkmaid.
Birket Foster

JOHN MILTON (1608–1674)

65

To the Botanic Muse

from: The Botanic Garden

Descend, ye hovering sylphs! aerial choirs,
And sweep with little hands your silver lyres;
With fairy footsteps print your grassy rings,
Ye gnomes! accordant to the tinkling strings:
While in soft notes I tune to oaten reed
Gay hopes, and amorous sorrows of the mead.
From giant oaks, that wave their branches dark,
To the dwarf moss that clings upon their bark,
What beaux and beauties crowd the gaudy groves,
And woo and win their vegetable loves.
How snowdrops cold, and blue-eyed harebells blend
Their tender tears, as o'er the stream they bend;
The lovesick violet, and the primrose pale,
Bow their sweet heads, and whisper to the gale;
With secret sighs the virgin lily droops,
And jealous cowslips hang their tawny cups.
How the young rose in beauty's damask pride
Drinks the warm blushes of his bashful bride;
With honied lips enamoured woodbines meet,
Clasp with fond arms, and mix their kisses sweet.

Sweet Summer Time. *Richard Redgrave*

Stay thy soft-murmuring waters, gentle rill;
Hush, whispering winds; ye rustling leaves be still;
Rest, silver butterflies, your quivering wings;
Alight, ye beetles, from your airy rings;
Ye painted moths, your gold-eyed plumage furl,
Bow your wide horns, your spiral trunks uncurl;
Glitter, ye glow-worms, on your mossy beds;
Descend, ye spiders, on your lengthened threads;
Slide here, ye horned snails, with varnished shells;
Ye bee-nymphs, listen in your waxen cells!

Botanic Muse! who in this latter age
Led by your airy hand the Swedish sage,
Bade his keen eye your secret haunts explore
On dewy dell, high wood, and winding shore;
Say on each leaf how tiny Graces dwell;
How laugh the Pleasures in a blossom's bell;
How insect Loves arise on cobweb wings,
Aim their light shafts, and point their little stings.

ERASMUS DARWIN (1731–1802)

Cray Fields. *Graham Sutherland*

Summer

Winter is cold-hearted,
    Spring is yea and nay,
Autumn is a weathercock
    Blown every way.
    Summer days for me
When every leaf is on its tree;

    When Robin's not a beggar,
    And Jenny Wren's a bride,
And larks hang singing, singing, singing
    Over the wheat-fields wide,
    And anchored lilies ride,
    And the pendulum spider
    Swings from side to side.

And blue-black beetles transact business,
    And gnats fly in a host,
And furry caterpillars hasten
    That no time be lost,
    And moths grow fat and thrive,
    And ladybirds arrive.

    Before green apples blush,
    Before green nuts embrown,
    Why, one day in the country
    Is worth one month in town;
    Is worth a day and a year
Of the dusty, musty, lag-last fashion
    That days drone elsewhere.

CHRISTINA ROSSETTI (1830–1894)

The naturalist's
Summer-evening walk

When day, declining, sheds a milder gleam,
What time the May-fly haunts the pool or stream;
When the still Owl skims round the grassy mead,
What time the timorous Hare limps forth to feed;
Then be the time to steal adown the dale,
And listen to the vagrant Cuckoo's tale;
To hear the clamorous Curlew call his mate,
Or the soft Quail his tender pain relate;
To see the Swallow sweep the darkening plain
Belated, to support her infant train;
To mark the Swift in rapid giddy ring
Dash round the steeple, unsubdued of wing:
Amusive birds! say where your hid retreat
When the frost rages and the tempests beat;
Whence your return, by such nice instinct led,
When Spring, soft season, lifts her bloomy head?
Such baffled searches mock man's prying pride,
The GOD of Nature is your secret guide!
While deepening shades obscure the face of day,
To yonder bench leaf-sheltered let us stray,
Till blended objects fail the swimming sight,
And all the fading landscape sinks in night;
To hear the drowsy Dor come brushing by
With buzzing wing, or the shrill Cricket cry;
To see the feeding Bat glance through the wood;
To catch the distant falling of the flood;
While o'er the cliff th' awakened Churn-owl hung
Through the still gloom protracts his chattering song;
While high in air, and poised upon his wings
Unseen, the soft enamour'd Wood-lark sings:
These, Nature's works, the curious mind employ,
Inspire a soothing, melancholy joy:
As fancy warms, a pleasing kind of pain
Steals o'er the cheek, and thrills the creeping vein!

Each rural sight, each sound, each smell, combine;
The tinkling sheep-bell, or the breath of kine;
The new-mown hay that scents the swelling breeze,
Or cottage-chimney smoking through the trees,
The chilling night-dews fall:—away, retire;—
For see, the Glow-worm lights her amorous fire!
Thus, ere night's veil had half-obscur'd the sky,
Th'impatient damsel hung her lamp on high:
True to the signal, by love's meteor led,
Leander hastened to his Hero's bed.

GILBERT WHITE (1720–1793)

Selborne

That quiet vale! it greets my vision now,
  As when we saw it, one autumnal day,
  A cloudless sun brightening each feathery spray
Of woods that clothed the Hanger to its brow:
Woods, whose luxuriance hardly might allow
  A peep at that small hamlet, as it lay,
  Bosom'd in orchard-plots and gardens gay,
With here and there a field, perchance, to plough.
Delightful valley! still I own thy claim;
  As when I gave thee one last lingering look,
  And felt thou wast indeed a fitting nook
For him to dwell in, whose undying name
Has unto thee bequeath'd its humble fame,
  Pure, and imperishable,—like his book!

BERNARD BARTON (1784–1849)

Tree Trunk. *Harold Gilman*

The wood of August

The wood gathers strength of green in mid August
Calling from the deep all store of April water
And later, to be triumphant while the time serves;
Golden rod, orchis, guilder rose and scabious
Grow near him, and he watches the three swerve
Of Cotswold Edge, South Severn and Malvern Sideways.
Soon he will change, the nuts will ripen, and tideways
Turn greater to the equinox, and brown and brittle
His leaves save the little will change, and he'll dream
Of two things: how in rich music is fixed his glow:
(Ruddy and bronze), and in All-Hallow his August title
With vanished days to it, is held as high as any
(Poor un-named English Company)
That haws last through November and dare winter's battle.

IVOR GURNEY (1890–1937)

from:

The country walk

I am resolved, this charming day,
In the open field to stray;
And have no roof above my head,
But that whereon the gods do tread.
Before the yellow barn I see
A beautiful variety
Of strutting cocks, advancing stout,
And flirting empty chaff about,
Hens, ducks, and geese, and all their brood,
And turkeys gobbling for their food;
While rustics thrash the wealthy floor,
And tempt them all to crowd the door.

JOHN DYER (1699–1758)

The peninsula

When you have nothing more to say, just drive
For a day all round the peninsula.
The sky is tall as over a runway,
The land without marks so you will not arrive

But pass through, though always skirting landfall.
At dusk, horizons drink down sea and hill,
The ploughed field swallows the whitewashed gable
And you're in the dark again. Now recall

The glazed foreshore and silhouetted log,
That rock where breakers shredded into rags,
The leggy birds stilted on their own legs,
Islands riding themselves out into the fog

And drive back home, still with nothing to say
Except that now you will uncode all landscapes
By this: things founded clean on their own shapes,
Water and ground in their extremity.

SEAMUS HEANEY (1939-)

In The Fens

Wandering by the river's edge,
I love to rustle through the sedge,
And through the woods of reed to tear
Almost as high as bushes are.
Yet, turning quick with shudder chill,
As danger ever does from ill,
Fear's moment-ague quakes the blood,
While plop the snake coils in the flood
And, hissing with a forkèd tongue,
Across the river winds along.
In coat of orange, green, and blue
Now on a willow branch I view,
Grey waving to the sunny gleam,
Kingfishers watch the ripple stream
For little fish that nimble by
And in the gravel shallows lie.
Eddies run before the boats,
Gurgling where the fisher floats,
Who takes advantage of the gale
And hoists his handkerchief for sail
On osier twigs that form a mast—
And quick his nutshell hurries past,
While idly lies, nor wanted more,
The sprit that pushed him on before.
There's not a hill in all the view,
Save that a forkèd cloud or two
Upon the verge of distance lies
And into mountains cheats the eyes....

JOHN CLARE (1793–1864)

May in the green-wood

In somer when the shawes by sheyne,
   And leves be large and long,
Hit is full merry in feyre foreste
   To here the foulys song.

To se the dere draw to the dale
   And leve the hilles hee,
And shadow him in the leves grene
   Under the green-wode tree.

Hit befell on Whitsontide
   Early in a May mornyng,
The Sonne up faire can shyne,
   And the briddis mery can syng.

'This is a mery mornyng,' said Litulle Johne;
   'Be Hym that dyed on tre;
A more mery man than I am one
   Lyves not in Christiantè.

'Pluk up thi hert, my dere mayster,'
   Litulle Johne can say,
'And thynk hit is a fulle fayre tyme
   In a mornynge of May.'

ANONYMOUS

Study of Trees. *John Crome*

Troubles of the day

As there, along the elmy hedge, I go
  By banksides white with parsley – parsley-bloom —
Where smell of new-mown hay comes wafted by
  On wind of dewy evening, evening gloom,
And homeward take my shaded way between
The hedge's high-tipp'd wood, and barley green,
      I sing, or mean
'O troubles of the day, flee to the west,
Come not my homeward way. I seek my rest.'

The dairy cows, by meadow trees, lie free
  Of calls to milkers' pails — the milkmaids' calls;
The horses now have left their rolling wheels
  And reel'd in home to stable, to their stalls,
And down the grey-pool'd stream the fish awhile
Are free from all the prowling angler's guile,
      And o'er the stile
I sink, and sing or say, 'Flee to the west,
O troubles of the day. I seek my rest.'

My boy — whose little high-rigged boat, athwart
  The windy pool, by day, at afternoon,
Has fluttered, tippling like a bird
  That tries to fly unfledged, to fly too soon —
Now sleeps forgetful of the boat, and fond
Old dog that he has taught to swim the pond.
      So flee beyond
The edge of sinking day, towards the west,
Ye troubles, flee away. I seek my rest.

A star is o'er the tower on the hill
    Whence rings no clanging knell, no evening peal;
The mill stands dark beside the flouncing foam,
    But still is all its gear, its mossy wheel.
No rooks now sweep along the darkened sky,
And o'er the road few feet or wheels go by.
            So fly, O fly
Ye troubles, with the day, adown the west,
Come not along my way. I seek my rest.

WILLIAM BARNES (1801–1886)

Summer afternoon

Far off the rook, tired by the mid-day beam,
    Caws lazily this summer afternoon;
    The butterflies, with wandering up and down
O'er flower-bright marsh and meadow, wearied seem;
With vacant gaze, lost in a waking dream,
    We, listless, on the busy insects pore,
    In rapid dance uncertain, darting o'er
The smooth-spread surface of the tepid stream;
The air is slothful, and will scarce convey
    Soft sounds of idle waters to the ear;
    In brightly-dim obscurity appear
The distant hills which skirt the landscape gay;
While restless fancy owns the unnerving sway
    In visions often changed, but nothing clear.

THOMAS DOUBLEDAY (1790–1870)

The squirrel-hunt

Then, as a nimble Squirrel from the wood,
Ranging the hedges for his filbert-food,
Sits partly on a bough his browne nuts cracking,
And from the shell the sweet white kernell taking,
Till (with their crookes and bags) a sort of boyes,
(To share with him) come with so great a noyse,
That he is forc'd to leave a nut nigh broke,
And for his life leape to a neighbour oake;
Thence to a beeche, thence to a row of ashes;
Whilst through the quagmires, and red water plashes,
The boyes runne dabling through thicke and thin,
One tears his hose, another breakes his shin:
This, torn and tatter'd, hath with much adoe
Got by the bryers; and that hath lost his shoe;
This drops his hand; that headlong falls for haste;
Another cryes behinde for being last;
With stickes and stones, and many a sounding hollow,
The little foole, with no small sport, they follow,
Whilst he, from tree to tree, from spray to spray,
Gets to the wood, and hides him in his dray.

WILLIAM BROWNE (1591–1643)

The poplar-field

The poplars are felled, farewell to the shade
And the whispering sound of the cool colonnade,
The winds play no longer, and sing in the leaves,
Nor Ouse on his bosom their image receives.

Twelve years have elapsed since I first took a view
Of my favourite field and the bank where they grew,
And now in the grass behold they are laid,
And the tree is my seat that once lent me a shade.

The blackbird has fled to another retreat
Where the hazels afford him a screen from the heat,
And the scene where his melody charmed me before,
Resounds with his sweet-flowing ditty no more.

My fugitive years are all hasting away,
And I must ere long lie as lowly as they,
With a turf on my breast, and a stone at my head,
Ere another such grove shall arise in its stead.

'Tis a sight to engage me, if any thing can,
To muse on the perishing pleasures of man;
Though his life be a dream, his enjoyments, I see,
Have a being less durable even than he.

WILLIAM COWPER (1731–1800)

The midges dance aboon the burn

The midges dance aboon the burn;
   The dews begin to fa';
The pairtricks down the rushy holm
   Set up their e'ening ca'.
Now loud and clear the blackbird's sang
   Rings through the briary shaw,
While, flitting gay, the swallows play
   Around the castle wa'.

Beneath the golden gloamin' sky
   The mavis mends her lay;
The redbreast pours his sweetest strains
   To charm the lingering day;
While weary yeldrins seem to wail
   Their little nestlings torn,
The merry wren, frae den to den,
   Gaes jinking through the thorn.

The roses fauld their silken leaves,
   The foxglove shuts its bell;
The honeysuckle and the birk
   Spread fragrance through the dell.
Let others crowd the giddy court
   Of mirth and revelry,
The simple joys that nature yields
   Are dearer far to me.

ROBERT TANNAHILL (1774–1810)

Tempestuous June

from: Thyrsis

So, some tempestuous morn in early June,
   When the year's primal burst of bloom is o'er,
     Before the roses and the longest day —
   When garden-walks and all the grassy floor
     With blossoms red and white of fallen May
       And chestnut-flowers are strewn —
   So have I heard the cuckoo's parting cry,
     From the wet field, through the vext garden-trees,
     Come with the volleying rain and tossing breeze:
   The bloom is gone, and with the bloom go I!

MATTHEW ARNOLD (1822–1888)

Speak of the North

Speak of the North! A lonely moor
Silent and dark and trackless swells,
The waves of some wild streamlet pour
Hurriedly through its ferny dells.

Profoundly still the twilight air,
Lifeless the landscape; so we deem
Till like a phantom gliding near
A stag bends down to drink the stream.

And far away a mountain zone,
A cold, white waste of snow-drifts lies,
And one star, large and soft and lone,
Silently lights the unclouded skies.

CHARLOTTE BRONTË (1816–1855)

83

The Weald of Kent

from: The Land

The common saying goes, that on the hill
A man may lie in bed to work his farm,
Propping his elbows on his window-sill
To watch his harvest growing like a charm.
But the man who works the wet and weeping soil
Down in the Weald, must marl and delve and till
His three-horse land, fearing nor sweat nor droil.
For through the winter he must fight the flood,
The clay, that yellow enemy, that rots
His land, sucks at his horses' hooves
So that his waggon plunges in the mud,
And horses strain, but waggon never moves;
Delays his plough, and holds his spud
With yeavy spite in trenching garden-plots,
The catchy clay, that does its utmost harm,
And comes into his house, to spoil
Even his dwelling, creeps into his bones
Before their time, and makes them ache,
Leaving its token in his husky tones;
And all through summer he must see the clay
Harden as brick, and bake,
And open cracks to swallow up his arm,
Where neither harrow, hoe, nor rake
Can rasp a tilth, but young and eager shoots
Pierce into blank, and wither at the roots.
Yet with his stupid loyalty he will say,
Being a wealden man of wealden land,
Holding his wealden honour as a pledge,
'In times of drought those farms up on the ridge,
Light soil, half sand,
With the first summer gale blow half away,'
And lifts his eye towards the hill with scorn.

Kentish Landscape. *J. E. Millais*

But only a bold man ploughs the Weald for corn,
Most are content with fruit or pasture, knowing
Too well both drought and winter's heavy going;
So the lush Weald to-day
Lies green in distance, and the horizon's sweep
Deepens to blue in woods, with pointed spire
Pricking the foreground by the village tiles,
And the hop-kiln's whitened chimney stares between
Paler and darker green of Kentish miles,
And rarely a patch of corn in metal fire
Burnished by sunset ruffles in the green;
But meadow, shaw, and orchard keep
The glaucous country like a hilly sea
Pure in its monotone.

V. SACKVILLE-WEST (1892–1962)

from

The Old Vicarage, Grantchester

Ah God! to see the branches stir
Across the moon at Grantchester!
To smell the thrilling-sweet and rotten
Unforgettable, unforgotten
River-smell, and hear the breeze
Sobbing in the little trees.
Say, do the elm-clumps greatly stand
Still guardians of that holy land?
The chestnuts shade, in reverend dream,
The yet unacademic stream?
Is dawn a secret shy and cold
Anadyomene, silver-gold?
And sunset still a golden sea
From Haslingfield to Madingley?
And after, ere the night is born,
Do hares come out about the corn?
Oh, is the water sweet and cool,
Gentle and brown, above the pool?
And laughs the immortal river still
Under the mill, under the mill?
Say, is there Beauty yet to find?
And Certainty? and Quiet kind?
Deep meadows yet, for to forget
The lies, and truths, and pain? ... oh! yet
Stands the Church clock at ten to three?
And is there honey still for tea?

RUPERT BROOKE (1887–1915)

Woodland scenery

His task had Giles, in fields remote from home;
Oft has he wish'd the rosy morn to come:
And when at day-break summon'd from his bed,
Light as the lark that carol'd o'er his head;
His sandy way, deep-worn by hasty showers,
O'er-arch'd with oaks that form'd fantastic bowers,
Waving aloft their towering branches proud,
In borrow'd tinges from the eastern cloud,
(When inspiration, pure as ever flow'd,
And genuine transport in his bosom glow'd,)
His own shrill matin join'd the various notes
Of Nature's music, from a thousand throats:
The blackbird strove with emulation sweet,
And echo answer'd from her close retreat;
The sporting white-throat on some twig's end borne,
Pour'd hymns to freedom and the rising morn;
Stopp'd in her song, perchance, the starting thrush
Shook a white shower from the black-thorn bush,
Where dewdrops thick as early blossoms hung,
And trembled as the minstrel sweetly sung:
Across his path, in either grove to hide,
The timid rabbit scouted by his side;
Or bold cock pheasant stalk'd along the road,
Whose gold and purple tints alternate glow'd.

ROBERT BLOOMFIELD (1766–1823)

Overleaf: Cornard Wood. *Thomas Gainsborough*

Signs of rain

The hollow winds begin to blow,
The clouds look black, the glass is low,
The soot falls down, the spaniels sleep,
And spiders from their cobwebs peep:
Last night the sun went pale to bed,
The moon in halos hid her head.
The boding shepherd heaves a sigh,
For see! a rainbow spans the sky:
The walls are damp, the ditches smell,
Clos'd is the pink-eyed pimpernel.
Hark! how the chairs and tables crack;
Old Betty's joints are on the rack;
Loud quack the ducks, the peacocks cry,
The distant hills are seeming nigh.
How restless are the snorting swine, —
The busy flies disturb the kine.
Low o'er the grass the swallow wings;
The cricket too, how loud it sings;
Puss on the hearth, with velvet paws,
Sits smoothing o'er her whisker'd jaws.
Through the clear stream the fishes rise,
And nimbly catch the incautious flies.
The sheep were seen at early light
Cropping the meads with eager bite.
Though June, the air is cold and chill;
The mellow black-bird's voice is still.
The glow-worms, numerous and bright,
Illum'd the dewy dell last night.
At dusk the squalid toad was seen,
Hopping, and crawling, o'er the green.
The frog has lost his yellow vest,
And in a dingy suit is dress'd.
The leech, disturb'd, is dewly risen,
Quite to the summit of his prison.

The whirling winds the dust obeys,
And in the rapid eddy plays;
My dog, so alter'd in his taste,
Quits mutton-bones on grass to feast;
And see yon rooks, how odd their flight,
They imitate the gliding kite,
Or seem precipitate to fall,
As if they felt the piercing ball:—
'Twill surely rain,—I see with sorrow;
Our jaunt must be put off to-morrow.

CHARLES JENNER (1736–1774)

To Daisies, not to shut so soone

Shut not so soon; the dull-ey'd night
  Has not as yet begunne
To make a seizure on the light,
  Or to seale up the Sun.

No marigolds yet closèd are;
  No shadowes great appeare;
Nor doth the early Shepheards Starre
  Shine like a spangle here.

Stay but till my *Julia* close
  Her life-begetting eye;
And let the whole world then dispose
  It selfe to live or dye.

ROBERT HERRICK (1591–1674)

To the skylark

Ethereal Minstrel! Pilgrim of the sky!
Dost thou despise the earth where cares abound?
Or, while the wings aspire, are heart and eye
Both with thy nest upon the dewy ground?
Thy nest which thou canst drop into at will
Those quivering wings composed, that music still!

To the last point of vision, and beyond,
Mount, daring Warbler! that love-prompted strain,
('Twixt thee and thine a never-failing bond)
Thrills not the less the bosom of the plain:

Yet might'st thou seem, proud privilege! to sing
All independent of the leafy spring.

Leave to the Nightingale her shady wood;
A privacy of glorious light is thine;
Whence thou dost pour upon the world a flood
Of harmony, with instinct more divine;
Type of the wise who soar, but never roam;
True to the kindred points of Heaven and Home!

WILLIAM WORDSWORTH (1770–1850)

The Skylark. *Samuel Palmer*

Larches

Larches are most fitting to small red hills
That rise like swollen ant-heaps likeably
And modest before big things like near Malvern
Or Cotswold's farther early Italian
Blue arrangement, unassuming as the
Cowslip, celandines, buglewort and daisies
That trinket out the green swerves like a child's game.
O, never so careless or lavish as here ...

IVOR GURNEY (1890–1937)

Cowslips and Larks

I hear it said yon land is poor,
In spite of those rich cowslips there—
And all the singing larks it shoots
To heaven from the cowslips' roots.
But I, with eyes that beauty find,
And music ever in my mind,
Feed my thoughts well upon that grass
Which starves the horse, the ox, and ass.
So here I stand, two miles to come
To Shapwick and my ten-days-home,
Taking my summer's joy, although
The distant clouds are dark and low,
And comes a storm that, fierce and strong,
Has brought the Mendip Hills along:
Those hills that, when the light is there,
Are many a sunny mile from here.

W. H. DAVIES (1871–1940)

Nightingales' song

from: Prometheus Unbound

There the voluptuous nightingales,
   Are awake through all the broad noonday.
When one with bliss or sadness fails,
   And through the windless ivy-boughs,
   Sick with sweet love, droops dying away
On its mate's music-panting bosom;
Another from the swinging blossom,
   Watching to catch the languid close
   Of the last strain, then lifts on high
   The wings of the weak melody,
'Till some new strain of feeling bear
   The song, and all the woods are mute;
When there is heard through the dim air
The rush of wings, and rising there
   Like many a lake-surrounded flute,
Sounds overflow the listener's brain
So sweet, that joy is almost pain.

PERCY BYSSHE SHELLEY (1792–1822)

The coast: Norfolk

As on the highway's quiet edge
He mows the grass beside the hedge,
The old man has for company
The distant, grey, salt-smelling sea,
A poppied field, a cow and calf,
The finches on the telegraph.

Hung on his faded back a hone,
He slowly, slowly, scythes alone
In silence of the wind-soft air,
With ladies' bedstraw everywhere,
With whitened corn, and tarry poles,
And far-off gulls like risen souls.

FRANCES CORNFORD (1886–1960)

A contemplation upon flowers

Brave flowers, that I could gallant it like you
And be as little vain,
You come abroad, and make a harmless show,
And to your beds of earth again;
You are not proud, you know your birth
For your embroidered garments are from earth:

You do obey your months, and times, but I
Would have it ever spring,
My fate would know no winter, never die
Nor think of such a thing;
Oh that I could my bed of earth but view
And smile, and look as cheerfully as you:

O teach me to see death, and not to fear
But rather to take truce:
How often have I seen you at a bier,
And there look fresh and spruce;
You fragrant flowers, then teach me that my breath
Like yours may sweeten, and perfume my death.

HENRY KING (1592–1669)

Bellrope Meadow. *Stanley Spencer*

Fulfilment

Now came fulfilment of the year's desire;
The tall wheat, coloured by the August fire,
Grew heavy-headed, dreading its decay,
And blacker grew the elm-trees day by day.
About the edges of the yellow corn,
And o'er the gardens grown somewhat outworn
The bees went hurrying to fill up their store;
The apple-boughs bent over more and more;
With peach and apricot the garden wall
Was odorous, and the pears began to fall
From off the high tree with each freshening breeze.

WILLIAM MORRIS (1834–1896)

The Hayfield. *F. M. Brown*

Upper Lambourn

Up the ash-tree climbs the ivy,
    Up the ivy climbs the sun,
With a twenty-thousand pattering
    Has a valley breeze begun,
Feathery ash, neglected elder,
    Shift the shade and make it run —

Shift the shade toward the nettles,
    And the nettles set it free
To streak the stained Carrara headstone
    Where, in nineteen-twenty-three,
He who trained a hundred winners
    Paid the Final Entrance Fee.

Leathery limbs of Upper Lambourn,
    Leathery skin from sun and wind,
Leathery breeches, spreading stables,
    Shining saddles left behind —
To the down the string of horses
    Moving out of sight and mind.

Feathery ash in leathery Lambourn
    Waves above the sarsen stone,
And Edwardian plantations
    So coniferously moan
As to make the swelling downland,
    Far-surrounding, seem their own.

JOHN BETJEMAN (1906–   )

Summer Evening. *David Lucas after John Constable*

Summer evening

The frog, half fearful, jumps across the path,
And little mouse that leaves its hole at eve
Nimbles with timid dread beneath the swath;
My rustling steps awhile their joys deceive,
Till past — and then the cricket sings more strong,
And grasshoppers in merry moods still wear
The short night weary with their fretting song.
Up from behind the mole-hill jumps the hare,
Cheat of his chosen bed, and from the bank
The yellow-hammer flutters in short fears
From off its nest hid in the grasses rank,
And drops again when no more noise it hears.
Thus nature's human link and endless thrall,
Proud man, still seems the enemy of all.

JOHN CLARE (1793–1864)

Evening's close

from: The Deserted Village

Sweet was the sound when oft at evening's close,
Up yonder hill the village murmur rose;
There as I past with careless steps and slow,
The mingling notes came softened from below;
The swain responsive as the milk-maid sung,
The sober herd that lowed to meet their young,
The noisy geese that gabbled o'er the pool,
The playful children just let loose from school,
The watch-dog's voice that bayed the whispering wind,
And the loud laugh that spoke the vacant mind,
These all in sweet confusion sought the shade,
And filled each pause the nightingale had made.

OLIVER GOLDSMITH (1728–1774)

Shakespeare's Cliff

from: King Lear

Heere's the place: stand still: how fearefull
And dizzie 'tis, to cast one's eyes so low,
The Crowes and Choughes, that wing the midway ayre
Show scarce so grosse as Beetles. Halfe way downe
Hangs one that gathers Sampire: dreadful Trade:
Me thinkes he seemes no bigger than his head.
The Fishermen, that walke upon the beach
Appeare like Mice: and yond tall Anchoring Barke,
Diminish'd to her Cocke: her Cocke, a Buoy
Almost too small for sight. The murmuring Surge,
That on the unnumbered idle Pebbles chafes
Cannot be heard so high. Ile look no more,
Least my braine turne, and the deficient sight
Topple downe headlong.

WILLIAM SHAKESPEARE (1564–1616)

Suffolk heathland

from: The Village

Lo! where the heath, with withering brake grown o'er,
Lends the light turf that warms the neighbouring poor;
From thence a length of burning sand appears,
Where the thin harvest waves its wither'd ears;
Rank weeds, that ever art and care defy,
Reign o'er the land, and rob the blighted rye:
There thistles stretch their prickly arms afar,
And to the ragged infant threaten war;
There poppies nodding, mock the hope of toil;
There the blue bugloss paints the sterile soil;
Hardy and high, above the slender sheaf,
The slimy mallow waves her silky leaf;
O'er the young shoot the charlock throws a shade,
And clasping tares cling round the sickly blade;
With mingled tints the rocky coasts abound,
And a sad splendour vainly shines around.

GEORGE CRABBE (1754–1832)

A farm picture

Through the ample open door of the peaceful country barn,
A sunlit pasture field with cattle and horses feeding,
And haze and vista, and the far horizon fading away.

WALT WHITMAN (1819–1892)

A Summer's evening

Clear had the day been from the dawn,
    All chequer'd was the sky,
Thin clouds, like scarfs of cobweb lawn,
    Veil'd Heaven's most glorious eye.

The winde had no more strength than this,
    That leisurely it blew,
To make one leaf the next to kiss
    That closely by it grew.

The rills that on the pebbles play'd
    Might now be heard at will;
This world they only music made,
    Else everything was still.

The flowers like brave embroidered girls,
    Look'd as they most desired
To see whose head with orient pearls
    Most curiously was tired;

And to itself the subtle air
    Such sovreignty assumes,
That it receiv'd too large a share
    From Nature's rich perfumes.

MICHAEL DRAYTON (1563–1631)

Panshanger Park. *Spencer Gore*

The end of Summer

from: Summer's Last Will and Testament

Fayre Summer droops, droope men and beasts therefore:
So fayre a summer looke for never more.
All good things vanish lesse then in a day,
Peace, plenty, pleasure sodainely decay.
    Goe not yet away bright soule of the sad yeare,
    The earth is hell when thou leav'st to appeare.

What, shall those flowres, that deckt thy garland erst,
Upon thy grave be wastfully disperst?
O trees, consume your sap in sorrowes sourse.
Streames, turne to teares your tributary course.
    Go not yet hence, bright soule of the sad yeare.
    The earth is hell, when thou leav'st to appeare.

THOMAS NASH (1567–1601)

Escape from the city

To one who has been long in city pent,
   'Tis very sweet to look into the fair
   And open face of heaven, — to breathe a prayer
Full in the smile of the blue firmament.
Who is more happy, when, with heart's content,
   Fatigued he sinks into some pleasant lair
   Of wavy grass, and reads a debonair
And gentle tale of love and languishment?
Returning home at evening, with an ear
   Catching the notes of Philomel, — an eye
Watching the sailing cloudlet's bright career,
   He mourns that day so soon has glided by:
E'en like the passage of an angel's tear
   That falls through the clear ether silently.

JOHN KEATS (1795–1821)

Beside the Thames

from: Thyrsis

I know these slopes; who knows them if not I?—
   But many a dingle on the loved hill-side,
     With thorns once studded, old, white-blossom'd trees,
   Where thick the cowslips grew, and far descried
     High tower'd the spikes of purple orchises,
      Hath since our day put by
   The coronals of that forgotten time;
     Down each green bank hath gone the ploughboy's team,
     And only in the hidden brookside gleam
Primroses, orphans of the flowery prime.

MATTHEW ARNOLD (1822–1888)

Banbury Chap-Book

The Harvest Moon

The flame-red moon, the harvest moon,
Rolls along the hills, gently bouncing,
A vast balloon,
Till it takes off, and sinks upward
To lie in the bottom of the sky, like a gold doubloon.

The harvest moon has come,
Booming softly through heaven, like a bassoon.
And earth replies all night, like a deep drum.

So people can't sleep,
So they go out where elms and oak trees keep
A kneeling vigil, in a religious hush.
The harvest moon has come!

And all the moonlit cows and all the sheep
Stare up at her petrified, while she swells
Filling heaven, as if red hot, and sailing
Closer and closer like the end of the world.

Till the gold fields of stiff wheat
Cry 'We are ripe, reap us!' and the rivers
Sweat from the melting hills.

TED HUGHES (1930–   )

By the side of Rydal Mere

The linnet's warble, sinking towards a close,
Hints to the thrush 'tis time for their repose;
The shrill-voiced thrush is heedless, and again
The monitor revives his old sweet strain;
But both will soon be mastered, and the copse
Be left as silent as the mountain-tops,
Ere some commanding star dismiss to rest
The throng of rooks, that now, from twig or nest,
(After a steady flight on home-bound wings,
And a last game of mazy hoverings
Around their ancient grove) with cawing noise
Disturb the liquid music's equipoise.

O Nightingale! Who ever heard thy song
Might here be moved, till Fancy grows so strong
That listening sense is pardonably cheated
Where wood or stream by thee was never greeted.
Surely, from fairest spots of favoured lands,
Were not some gifts withheld by jealous hands,
This hour of deepening darkness here would be
As a fresh morning for new harmony;
And lays as prompt would hail the dawn of Night:
A *dawn* she has both beautiful and bright,
When the East kindles with the full moon's light;
Not like the rising sun's impatient glow
Dazzling the mountains, but an overflow
Of solemn splendour, in mutation slow.
    Wanderer by spring with gradual progress led,
For sway profoundly felt as widely spread;
To king, to peasant, to rough sailor, dear,
And to the soldier's trumpet-wearied ear;
How welcome wouldst thou be to this green Vale
Fairer than Tempe! Yet, sweet Nightingale!
From the warm breeze that bears thee on, alight
At will, and stay thy migratory flight;
Build, at thy choice, or sing, by pool or fount,
Who shall complain, or call thee to account?
The wisest, happiest, of our kind are they
That ever walk content with Nature's way,
God's goodness—measuring bounty as it may;
For whom the gravest thought of what they miss,
Chastening the fulness of a present bliss,
Is with that wholesome office satisfied,
While unrepining sadness is allied
In thankful bosoms to a modest pride.

WILLIAM WORDSWORTH (1770–1850)

Rydal Lake. *Edward Finden after William Westall*

Sussex 1902

God gave all men all earth to love,
    But, since our hearts are small,
Ordained for each one spot should prove
    Belovèd over all;
That, as He watched Creation's birth,
    So we, in godlike mood,
May of our love create our earth
    And see that it is good.

So one shall Baltic pines content,
    As one some Surrey glade,
Or one the palm-grove's droned lament
    Before Levuka's Trade.
Each to his choice, and I rejoice
    The lot has fallen to me
In a fair ground—in a fair ground—
    Yea, Sussex by the sea!

No tender-hearted garden crowns,
    No bosomed woods adorn
Our blunt, bow-headed, whale-backed Downs,
    But gnarled and writhen thorn—
Bare slopes where chasing shadows skim,
    And, through the gaps revealed,
Belt upon belt, the wooded, dim,
    Blue goodness of the Weald.

Clean of officious fence or hedge,
    Half-wild and wholly tame,
The wise turf cloaks the white cliff-edge
    As when the Romans came.
What sign of those that fought and died
    At shift of sword and sword?
The barrow and the camp abide,
    The sunlight and the sward.

Here leaps ashore the full Sou'west
  All heavy-winged with brine,
Here lies above the folded crest
  The Channel's leaden line;
And here the sea-fogs lap and cling,
  And here, each warning each,
The sheep-bells and the ship-bells ring
  Along the hidden beach.

We have no waters to delight
  Our broad and brookless vales—
Only the dewpond on the height
  Unfed, that never fails—
Whereby no tattered herbage tells
  Which way the season flies—
Only our close-bit thyme that smells
  Like dawn in Paradise.

Here through the strong and shadeless days
  The tinkling silence thrills;
Or little, lost, Down churches praise
  The Lord who made the hills:
But here the Old Gods guard their round,
  And, in her secret heart,
The heathen kingdom Wilfrid found
  Dreams, as she dwells, apart.

Though all the rest were all my share,
  With equal soul I'd see
Her nine-and-thirty sisters fair,
  Yet none more fair than she.
Choose ye your need from Thames to Tweed,
  And I will choose instead
Such lands as lie 'twixt Rake and Rye,
  Black Down and Beachy Head.

I will go out against the sun
    Where the rolled scarp retires,
And the Long Man of Wilmington
    Looks naked toward the shires;
And east till doubling Rother crawls
    To find the fickle tide,
By dry and sea-forgotten walls,
    Our ports of stranded pride.

I will go north about the shaws
    And the deep ghylls that breed
Huge oaks and old, the which we hold
    No more than Sussex weed;
Or south where windy Piddinghoe's
    Begilded dolphin veers,
And red beside wide-bankèd Ouse
    Lie down our Sussex steers.

So to the land our hearts we give
    Till the sure magic strike,
And Memory, Use, and Love make live
    Us and our fields alike—
That deeper than our speech and thought,
    Beyond our reason's sway,
Clay of the pit whence we were wrought
    Yearns to its fellow-clay.

God gives all men, all earth to love,
    But, since man's heart is small,
Ordains for each one spot shall prove
    Belovèd over all.
Each to his choice, and I rejoice
    The lot has fallen to me
In a fair ground—in a fair ground—
    Yea, Sussex by the sea!

RUDYARD KIPLING (1865–1936)

The Sleeping Shepherd. *Samuel Palmer*

Harvest

from: August

Harvest approaches with its bustling day
The wheat tans brown and barley bleaches grey
In yellow garb the oat land intervenes
And tawney glooms the valley thronged with beans
Silent the village grows, wood wandering dreams
Seem not so lovely as its quiet seems
Doors are shut up as on a winters day
And not a child about them lies at play
The dust that winnows neath the breezes feet
Is all that stirs about the silent street
Fancy might think that desert spreading fear
Had whisperd terrors into quiets ear
Or plundering armys past the place had come
And drove the lost inhabitants from home
The fields now claim them where a motley crew
Of old and young their daily tasks pursue
The barleys beard is grey and wheat is brown
And wakens toil betimes to leave the town
The reapers leave their beds before the sun
And gleaners follow when home toils are done
To pick the littered ear the reaper leaves
And glean in open fields among the sheaves.

JOHN CLARE (1793–1864)

The Isle of Wight. *Richard Burchett*

To meadows

Ye have been fresh and green,
   Ye have been filled with flowers,
And ye the walks have been
   Where maids have spent their hours.

You have beheld how they
   With wicker arks did come
To kiss, and bear away
   The richer cowslips home.

You've heard them sweetly sing,
   And seen them in a round,
Each virgin like a spring
   With honeysuckles crowned.

But now we see none here
   Whose silvery feet did tread
And with dishevelled hair
   Adorned this smoother mead.

Like unthrifts having spent
   Your stock and needy grown,
You're left here to lament
   Your poor estates alone.

ROBERT HERRICK (1591–1674)

Near Stoke-by-Nayland. *Lionel Constable*

AUTUMN

Moonlight in Autumn

from: The Seasons

The Western Sun withdraws the shorten'd Day;
And humid Evening, gliding o'er the Sky,
In her chill Progress, to the Ground condens'd
The Vapours throws. Where creeping Waters ooze,
Where Marshes stagnate, and where Rivers wind,
Cluster the rolling Fogs, and swim along
The dusky-mantled Lawn. Mean-while the Moon
Full-orb'd, and breaking thro' the scatter'd Clouds,
Shews her broad Visage in the crimson'd East.
Turn'd to the Sun direct, her spotted Disk,
(Where Mountains rise, umbrageous Dales descend,
And Oceans roll, as optic Tube descries,)
A smaller Earth, gives all its Blaze again,
Void of its Flame, and sheds a softer Day.
Now thro' the passing Cloud she seems to stoop,
Now up the pure Cerulean rides sublime.
Wide the pale Deluge floats, and streaming mild
O'er the sky'd Mountain to the shadowy Vale,
While Rocks and Floods reflect the quivering Gleam,
The whole Air whitens with a boundless Tide
Of silver Radiance, trembling round the World.

The lengthen'd Night elaps'd, the Morning shines
Serene, in all her dewy Beauty bright,
Unfolding fair the last Autumnal Day.
And now the mounting Sun dispels the Fog;
The rigid Hoar-Frost melts before his Beam;
And hung on every Spray, on every Blade
Of Grass, the myriad Dew-Drops twinkle round.

JAMES THOMSON (1700–1748)

October

The green elm with the one great bough of gold
Lets leaves into the grass slip, one by one, —
The short hill grass, the mushrooms small, milk-white,
Harebell and scabious and tormentil,
That blackberry and gorse, in dew and sun,
Bow down to; and the wind travels too light
To shake the fallen birch leaves from the fern;
The gossamers wander at their own will.
At heavier steps than birds' the squirrels scold.
The rich scene has grown fresh again and new
As Spring and to the touch is not more cool
Than it is warm to the gaze; and now I might
As happy be as earth is beautiful,
Were I some other or with earth could turn
In alternation of violet and rose,
Harebell and snowdrop, at their season due,
And gorse that has no time not to be gay.
But if this be not happiness, — who knows?
Some day I shall think this a happy day,
And this mood by the name of melancholy
Shall no more blackened and obscurèd be.

EDWARD THOMAS (1878–1917)

A thunder-storm

The wind begun to rock the grass
With threatening tunes and low, —
He flung a menace at the earth,
A menace at the sky.

The leaves unhooked themselves from trees
And started all abroad;
The dust did scoop itself like hands
And throw away the road.

The wagons quickened on the streets,
The thunder hurried slow;
The lightning showed a yellow beak,
And then a livid claw.

The birds put up the bars to nests,
The cattle fled to barns;
There came one drop of giant rain,
And then, as if the hands

That held the dams had parted hold,
The waters wrecked the sky,
But overlooked my father's house,
Just quartering a tree.

EMILY DICKINSON (1830–1886)

Fall of the Year

When Grasshopper, chirping late,
Easing thus his merry heart,
Not from cares but over-joy
Tells that Summer's out of date,
Yet thereat no fears annoy
His blithe spirit — not one smart
For lost moments, wishes ill —
As he sang so sings he still;
In his life-dregs keeping holy
That joy-essence fresh and clear,
Free from taint of melancholy,
Which from Nature, when the Year
Saw his birthday young like him,
He received, a boon of Glory
Man might envy, whom a whim —
A mere nothing — can o'er-dim . . .

When the Redbreast whistles blithe,
Taking of sweet song his fill,
Tho' the other birds be still;
And the lambs full-sized bleat strong,
Well-wool'd 'gainst the Winter's chill;
When no more the reaping-scythe
Finds a cornstalk to cut down,
And the stubble field looks brown
Where the formless vapour shows
Objects indistinct and wrong;
When the daylight shorter grows,
And owl's and bat's delight is long;
When, nigh eveless, Night draws on,
Waiting scarce for set of sun;
Like enchantress whose high spell
Works a sudden miracle . . .

When the peasant, weather-wise,
Shakes his grey head at the skies;
By his blazing cottage-flame
Mutters Winter's chilly name,
Lives o'er the past, in many a tale,
And prophesies, and quaffs his ale:
While in chimney-nook to sleep
Tired dog and urchin creep:

When the weather-signs are rife,
Telling of new Season's life;
And all creatures, instinct-wise,
Tho' taught not to philosophise,
Now prepare, each in his way,
To protect life's little day;
And thy own heart plainer still
Than falling leaf or faded hill,
Tells thee that the Summer's flown
With all joys that thou hast known ...

HENRY ELLISON (1811–1880)

The oak tree

The oak tree thrust its fist
Through the brown-paper wrapping of dry soil,
Letting light into the earth. Its wrist
Was rigged with segs, and stems of ivy
Wound varicose veins around the arm.
It opened its hand and birds flew to the fingers
As falcons to a falconer. A charm
Of chaffinch and linnet made tingle the thumbs of winter.
Spring brought gloves of green,
Summer itched with flies, and autumn
Doled out and dropped its pennies for the squirrels,
And the knuckles were wide to the wind. The lean
Old men goggled from the wood — brown snouts
Peeked from the ferns. Dandelions
Feathered their beards with seeds, and bramble knouts
Whipped their leather thighs, but they never felt them.

They shuffled up to the shins through paddock-stools and
    cow-pats,
And stood in a circle round the tree.
The oldest of them all (his beard
Draggled the ground like a weeping willow)
Touched never a stick, but three
Dropped the tree along the line he measured,
Lopped and topped the branches and ripped the bark off,
Till the wet trunk lay bare as a skinned rabbit. He
Drew out the pith and marrow of the log
And planed it thin as plywood. Shavings
Clog-danced on the cobbles, and yellow sawdust
Pollened the October grass.
He took the wood and bent it
Gently as a surgeon setting a broken bone,
But quick with a crack and a splitting of the spine
It snapped and lay dead in his hands. For a space he held it,
Surprised and sad, then (one arm pointing
Across the field to another tree) he threw it
Into a heaped fire of dead leaves
The men had kindled there. The tossed wood
Fell deep in the damp smoulder, till the slow smoke
Pushed up its fingers, gripping the skirts of the air.
And the hand of the fire was the hand of the living oak.

NORMAN NICHOLSON (1914–   )

A boy's song

Where the pools are bright and deep,
Where the grey trout lies asleep,
Up the river and o'er the lea,
That's the way for Billy and me.

Where the blackbird sings the latest,
Where the hawthorn blooms the sweetest,
Where the nestlings chirp and flee,
That's the way for Billy and me.

Where the mowers mow the cleanest,
Where the hay lies thick and greenest;
There to trace the homeward bee,
That's the way for Billy and me.

Where the hazel bank is steepest,
Where the shadow falls the deepest,
Where the clustering nuts fall free,
That's the way for Billy and me.

Why the boys should drive away
Little maidens from their play,
Or love to banter and fight so well,
That's the thing I never could tell.

But this I know, I love to play,
Through the meadow, among the hay:
Up the river and o'er the lea,
That's the way for Billy and me.

JAMES HOGG (1770–1835)

Dirge in woods

A wind sways the pines,
        And below
Not a breath of wild air;
Still as the mosses that glow
On the flooring and over the lines
Of the roots here and there.
The pine-tree drops its dead;
They are quiet, as under the seas.

Overhead, overhead
Rushes life in a race,
As the clouds the clouds chase;
        And we go,
And we drop like the fruits of the tree,
        Even we,
        Even so.

GEORGE MEREDITH (1828–1909)

Cambridgeshire

The stacks, like blunt impassive temples, rise
Across flat fields against the autumnal skies,
The hairy-hoovèd horses plough the land,
Or as in prayer and meditation stand
Upholding square, primeval, dung-stained carts,
With an unending patience in their hearts.

Nothing is changed. The farmer's gig goes by
Against the horizon. Surely, the same sky,
So vast and yet familiar, grey and mild,
And streaked with light like music, I, a child,
Lifted my face from leaf-edged lanes to see,
Late-coming home, to bread-and-butter tea.

FRANCES CORNFORD (1886–1960)

Reapers: Noonday Rest. *John Linnell*

Autumn Even-Song

The long cloud edged with streaming grey
    Soars from the West;
  The red leaf mounts with it away,
    Showing the nest
A blot among the branches bare:
There is a cry of outcasts in the air.

  Swift little breezes, darting chill,
    Pant down the lake;
  A crow flies from the yellow hill,
    And in its wake
A baffled line of labouring rooks:
Steel-surfaced to the light the river looks.

  Pale on the panes of the old hall
    Gleams the lone space
Between the sunset and the squall
    And on its face
Mournfully glimmers to the last:
Great oaks grow mighty minstrels in the blast.

  Pale the rain-rutted roadways shine
    In the green light
Behind the cedar and the pine:
    Come, thundering night!
  Blacken broad earth with hoards of storm:
For me yon valley-cottage beckons warm.

GEORGE MEREDITH (1828–1909)

Elegy written in a country churchyard

The Curfew tolls the knell of parting day,
The lowing herd wind slowly o'er the lea,
The plowman homeward plods his weary way,
And leaves the world to darkness and to me.

Now fades the glimmering landscape on the sight,
And all the air a solemn stillness holds,
Save where the beetle wheels his droning flight,
And drowsy tinklings lull the distant folds;

Save that from yonder ivy-mantled tow'r
The mopeing owl does to the moon complain
Of such, as wand'ring near her secret bow'r,
Molest her ancient solitary reign.

Beneath those rugged elms, that yew-tree's shade,
Where heaves the turf in many a mould'ring heap,
Each in his narrow cell for ever laid,
The rude Forefathers of the hamlet sleep.

The breezy call of incense-breathing Morn,
The swallow twitt'ring from the straw-built shed,
The cock's shrill clarion, or the echoing horn,
No more shall rouse them from their lowly bed.

For them no more the blazing hearth shall burn,
Or busy housewife ply her evening care:
No children run to lisp their sire's return,
Or climb his knees the envied kiss to share.

Oft did the harvest to their sickle yield,
Their furrow oft the stubborn glebe has broke;
How jocund did they drive their team afield!
How bow'd the woods beneath their sturdy stroke!

THOMAS GRAY (1716–1771)

The valley of seclusion

from: Reflections on having left a place of retirement

Low was our pretty Cot: our tallest Rose
Peeped at the chamber-window. We could hear
At silent noon, and eve, and early morn,
The Sea's faint murmur. In the open air
Our Myrtles blossomed; and across the porch
Thick Jasmins twined: the little landscape round
Was green and woody, and refreshed the eye.
It was a spot which you might aptly call
The Valley of Seclusion! Once I saw
(Hallowing his Sabbath-day by quietness)
A wealthy son of Commerce saunter by,
Bristowa's citizen: methought, it calmed
His thirst of idle gold, and made him muse
With wiser feelings: for he paused, and looked
With a pleased sadness, and gazed all around,
Then eyed our Cottage, and gazed round again,
And sighed, and said, it was a Blessed Place.
And we *were* blessed. Oft with patient ear
Long-listening to the viewless sky-lark's note
(Viewless, or haply for a moment seen
Gleaming on sunny wings) in whispered tones
I've said to my Beloved, 'Such, sweet Girl!
The inobtrusive song of Happiness,
Unearthly minstrelsy! then only heard
When the Soul seeks to hear; when all is hushed,
And the Heart listens!'

                But the time, when first
From that low Dell, steep up the stony Mount
I climbed with perilous toil and reached the top,
Oh! what a goodly scene! *Here* the bleak mount,
The bare bleak mountain speckled thin with sheep;
Grey clouds, that shadowing spot the sunny fields;
And river, now with bushy rocks o'er-browed,

Kerswell, Devon. *John White Abbott*

Now winding bright and full, with naked banks;
And seats, and lawns, the Abbey and the wood,
And cots, and hamlets, and faint city-spire;
The Channel *there*, the Islands and white sails,
Dim coasts, and cloud-like hills, and shoreless Ocean —
It seemed like Omnipresence! God, methought,
Had built him there a Temple: the whole World
Seemed *imaged* in its vast circumference:
No *wish* profaned my overwhelmed heart.
Blest hour! It was a luxury, — to be!

S. T. COLERIDGE (1772–1834)

Shoreham: twilight time

And now the trembling light
Glimmers behind the little hills and corn,
Ling'ring as loth to part; yet part thou must
And though than open day far pleasing more
(Ere yet the fields and pearlèd cups of flowers
    Twinkle in the parting light;)
Thee night shall hide, sweet visionary gleam
That softly lookest through the rising dew;
    Till all like silver bright,
    The faithful witness, pure and white,
    Shall look o'er yonder grassy hill,
    At this village, safe and still.
    All is safe and all is still,
    Save what noise the watch-dog makes
    Or the shrill cock the silence breaks.
    Now and then —
    And now and then —
    Hark! Once again,
    The wether's bell
    To us doth tell
Some little stirring in the fold.

Methinks the ling'ring dying ray
Of twilight time, doth seem more fair,
And lights the soul up more than day
When wide-spread sultry sunshines are:
Yet all is right and all most fair,
For thou, dear God, has formèd all;
Thou deckest every little flower,
Thou girdest every planet ball,
And mark'st when sparrows fall.

SAMUEL PALMER (1805–1881)

Folding the last Sheep. *Samuel Palmer*

Autumn

I love the fitful gust that shakes
    The casement all the day,
And from the mossy elm tree takes
    The faded leaves away,
Twirling them by the window pane
With thousand others down the lane.

I love to see the shaking twig
    Dance till the shut of eve,
The sparrow on the cottage rig,
    Whose chirp would make believe
That spring was just now flirting by
In summer's lap with flowers to lie.

I love to see the cottage smoke
    Curl upwards through the trees,
The pigeons nestled round the cote
    On November days like these;
The cock upon the dunghill crowing,
The mill-sails on the heath a-going.

JOHN CLARE (1793–1864)

The Cornfield Shelter. *John Linnell*

The bounty of Ceres

from: The Tempest

Ceres, most bounteous Lady, thy rich Leas
Of Wheate, Rye, Barley, Vetches, Oates and Pease;
Thy Turphie-Mountaines, where live nibling Sheepe,
And flat Medes thatchd with Stover, them to keepe:
Thy bankes with pioned, and twilled brims,
Which spungie Aprill, at thy hest betrims,
To make cold Nymphes chast crownes; and thy broome-
 groves,
Whose shadow the dismissed Batchelor loves,
Being lasse-lorne: thy pole-clipt vineyard,
And thy Sea-marge sterrile, and rockey-hard,
Where thou thy selfe do'st ayre, the Queene o'th Skie,
Whose watry Arch, and messenger, am I,
Bids thee leave these, and with her soveraigne grace,
Here on this grasse-plot, in this very place
To come, and sport: her Peacocks flye amaine:
Approach, rich *Ceres*, her to entertaine.

WILLIAM SHAKESPEARE (1564–1616)

The harvest field

There is nothing to note; only the mowers
Moving like doom. Slowly, one by one,
A gloom of bees rises and soon snores
Thunder-headed away into the sun.

Listen! Listen! do you hear the hiss
Of the scythe in the long grasses
That are silently tingling like bells that kiss
And repel as the wind passes?

There in the last care and core of corn
The hare is couched: not till the mowers flash
Their smiling scythes, and all its walls are shorn
Will the wild creature dash
Into the wintry air of hound and horn.

Listen! Listen! do you hear the hiss
Of the scythe in the long grasses of your laughter?
More is mowed than you know, for this
Is Time's swathe, and you are the one that he's after.

W. R. RODGERS (1909–1969)

Gleaning

Along the baulk the grasses drenched in dews
Soak through the morning gleaners' clumsy shoes,
And cloying cobwebs trammel their brown cheeks
While from the shouldering sun the dewfog reeks.
Now soon begun, on ground where yesterday
The rakers' warning-sheaf forbade their way,
Hard clacking dames in great white hoods make haste
To cram their lapbags with the barley waste,
Scrambling as if a thousand were but one,
Careless of stabbing thistles. Now the sun
Gulps up the dew and dries the stubs, and scores
Of tiny people trundle out of doors
Among the stiff stalks, where the scratched hands ply—
Red ants and blackamoors and such as fly;
Tunbellied, too, with legs a finger long,
The spider harvestman; the churlish strong
Black scorpion, prickled earwig, and that mite
Who shuts up like a leaden shot in fright
And lies for dead. And still before the rout
The young rats and the fieldmice whisk about
And from the trod whisp out the leveret darts,
Bawled at by boys that pass with blundering carts
Top-heavy to the red-tiled barns.—And still
The children feed their corn-sacks with good will,
And farmwives ever faster stoop and flounce.
The hawk drops down a plummet's speed to pounce
The nibbling mouse or resting lark away,
The lost mole tries to pierce the mattocked clay
In agony and terror of the sun.

The dinner hour and its grudged leisure won,
All sit below the pollards on the dykes,
Rasped with the twinge of creeping barley spikes.
Sweet beyond telling now the small beer goes

From the hooped hardwood bottles, the wasp knows,
And even hornets whizz from the eaten ash;
Then crusts are dropt and switches snatched to slash,
While safe in shadow of the apron thrown
Aside the bush which years before was grown
To snap the poacher's nets, the baby sleeps.

Now toil returns, in red-hot fluttering light,
And far afield the weary rabble creeps,
Oft happening blind wheat, black among the white,
That smutches where it touches quick as soot; —
Oft gaping where the landrail seems afoot,
Who with such magic throws his baffling speech
Far off he sounds when scarce beyond arm's reach.
The dogs are left to mind the morning's gain,
But squinting knaves can slouch to steal the grain.
Close to the farm the fields are gleaned agen,
Where the boy droves the turkey and white hen
To pick the shelled sweet corn, their hue and cry
Answers the gleaners' gabble; and sows trudge by
With little pigs to play and rootle there,
And all the fields are full of din and blare.

So steals the time past, so they glean and gloat;
The hobby-horse whirs round, the moth's dust coat
Blends with the stubble, scarlet soldiers fly
In airy pleasure; but the gleaners' eye
Sees little but their spoils, or robin-flower
Ever on tenterhooks to shun the shower, —
Their weather-prophet never known astray;
When he folds up, then towards the hedge glean they.
But now the dragon of the skies droops, pales,
And wandering in the wet grey western vales
Stumbles, and passes, and the gleaning's done.

The farmer with fat hares slung on his gun
Gives folks goodnight, as down the ruts they pull
The creaking two-wheeled handcarts bursting full,
And whimpering children cease their teazing squawls
While left alone the supping partridge calls—
Till all at home is stacked from mischief's way,
To thrash and dress the first wild windy day;
And each good wife crowns weariness with pride,
With such small winnings more than satisfied.

EDMUND BLUNDEN (1896–1974)

143

Autumn

A dirge

I

The warm sun is failing, the bleak wind is wailing,
The bare boughs are sighing, the pale flowers are dying,
    And the year
On the earth her death-bed, in a shroud of leaves dead,
    Is lying.
    Come, months, come away,
    From November to May,
    In your saddest array;
    Follow the bier
    Of the dead cold year,
And like dim shadows watch by her sepulchre.

II

The chill rain is falling, the nipt worm is crawling,
The rivers are swelling, the thunder is knelling
    For the year;
The blithe swallows are flown, and the lizards each gone
    To his dwelling;
    Come, months, come away;
    Put on white, black, and grey;
    Let your light sisters play —
    Ye, follow the bier
    Of the dead cold year,
And make her grave green with tear on tear.

PERCY BYSSHE SHELLEY (1792–1822)

Stray Rabbits. *Robert Collinson*

WINTER

Winter heavens

Sharp is the night, but stars with frost alive
Leap off the rim of earth across the dome.
It is a night to make the heavens our home
More than the nest whereto apace we strive.
Lengths down our road each fir-tree seems a hive,
Its swarms outrushing from the golden comb.
They waken waves of thoughts that burst to foam:
The living throb in me, the dead revive.
Yon mantle clothes us: there, past mortal breath,
Life glistens on the river of the death.
It folds us, flesh and dust; and have we knelt,
Or never knelt, or eyed as kine the springs
Of radiance, the radiance enrings:
And this is the soul's haven to have felt.

GEORGE MEREDITH (1828–1909)

The Teme at Downton. *Thomas Hearne*

Written on a bridge

When soft September brings again
  To yonder gorse its golden glow,
And Snowdon sends its autumn rain
  To bid thy current livelier flow;
Amid that ashen foliage light
When scarlet beads are glistering bright,
While alder boughs unchanged are seen
In summer livery of green;
When clouds before the cooler breeze
Are flying, white and large; with these
Returning, so may I return,
And find thee changeless, Pont-y-wern.

ARTHUR HUGH CLOUGH (1819–1861)

November

The mellow year is hastening to its close;
The little birds have almost sung their last,
Their small notes twitter in the dreary blast—
That shrill-piped harbinger of early snows;
The patient beauty of the scentless rose,
Oft with the morn's hoar crystal quaintly glass'd
Hangs, a pale mourner for the summer past,
And makes a little summer where it grows;
In the chill sunbeam of the faint brief day
The dusky waters shudder as they shine,
The russet leaves obstruct the straggling way
Of oozy brooks, which no deep banks define,
And the gaunt woods, in ragged, scant array,
Wrap their old limbs with sombre ivy twine.

HARTLEY COLERIDGE (1796–1849)

Inversnaid

This darksome burn, horseback brown,
His rollrock highroad roaring down,
In coop and in comb the fleece of his foam
Flutes and low to the lake falls home.

A windpuff-bonnet of fawn-froth
Turns and twindles over the broth
Of a pool so pitchblack, fell-frowning,
It rounds and rounds Despair to drowning.

Degged with dew, dappled with dew
Are the groins of the braes that the brook treads through,
Wiry heathpacks, flitches of fern,
And the beadbonny ash that sits over the burn.

What would the world be, once bereft
Of wet and wildness? Let them be left,
O let them be left, wildness and wet;
Long live the weeds and the wilderness yet.

GERARD MANLEY HOPKINS (1844–1889)

Weathers

I

This is the weather the cuckoo likes,
    And so do I;
When showers betumble the chestnut spikes,
    And nestlings fly:
And the little brown nightingale bills his best,
And they sit outside at 'The Travellers' Rest,'
And maids come forth sprig-muslin drest,
And citizens dream of the south and west,
    And so do I.

II

This is the weather the shepherd shuns,
    And so do I;
When beeches drip in browns and duns,
    And thresh, and ply;
And hill-hid tides throb, throe on throe,
And meadow rivulets overflow,
And drops on gate-bars hang in a row,
And rooks in families homeward go,
    And so do I.

THOMAS HARDY (1840–1928)

Under the mountain

Seen from above
The foam in the curving bay is a goose-quill
That feathers ... unfeathers ... itself.

Seen from above
The field is a flap and the haycocks buttons
To keep it flush with the earth.

Seen from above
The house is a silent gadget whose purpose
Was long since obsolete.

But when you get down
The breakers are cold scum and the wrack
Sizzles with stinking life.

When you get down
The field is a failed or worth-while crop, the source
Of back-ache if not heartache.

And when you get down
The house is a maelstrom of loves and hates where you —
Having got down — belong.

LOUIS MACNEICE (1907–1963)

Winter will follow

The heaving roses of the hedge are stirred
By the sweet breath of summer, and the bird
Makes from within his jocund voice be heard.

The winds that kiss the roses sweep the sea
Of uncut grass, whose billows rolling free
Half drown the hedges which part lea from lea.

But soon shall look the wondering roses down
Upon an empty field cut close and brown,
That lifts no more its height against their own.

And in a little while those roses bright,
Leaf after leaf, shall flutter from their height,
And on the reaped field lie pink and white.

And yet again the bird that sings so high
Shall ask the snow for alms with piteous cry,
Take fright in his bewildering bower, and die.

RICHARD WATSON DIXON (1833–1900)

Opening the Fold. *Samuel Palmer*

The Combe

The Combe was ever dark, ancient and dark.
Its mouth is stopped with bramble, thorn, and briar;
And no one scrambles over the sliding chalk
By beech and yew and perishing juniper
Down the half precipices of its sides, with roots
And rabbit holes for steps. The sun of Winter,
The moon of Summer, and all the singing birds
Except the missel-thrush that loves juniper,
Are quite shut out. But far more ancient and dark
The Combe looks since they killed the badger there,
Dug him out and gave him to the hounds,
That most ancient Briton of English beasts.

EDWARD THOMAS (1878–1917)

from:

February

The change has come at last, and from the west
Drives on the wind, and gives the clouds no rest,
And ruffles up the water thin that lies
Over the surface of the thawing ice;
Sunrise and sunset with no glorious show
Are seen, as late they were across the snow;
The wet-lipped west wind chilleth to the bone
More than the light and flickering east hath done.
Full soberly the earth's fresh hope begins,
Nor stays to think of what each new day wins:
And still it seems to bid us turn away
From this chill thaw to dream of blossomed May...

WILLIAM MORRIS (1834–1896)

Sea marsh

from: Peter Grimes

When tides were neap, and, in the sultry day,
Through the tall bounding mud-banks made their way,
Which on each side rose swelling, and below
The dark warm flood ran silently and slow:
There anchoring, Peter chose from man to hide,
There hang his head, and view the lazy tide
In its hot slimy channel slowly glide;
Where the small eels that left the deeper way
For the warm shore, within the shallows play;
Where gaping mussels, left upon the mud,
Slope their slow passage to the fallen flood:—
Here dull and hopeless he'd lie down and trace
How sidelong crabs had scrawl'd their crooked race;
Or sadly listen to the tuneless cry
Of fishing gull or clanging golden-eye;
What time the sea-birds to the marsh would come,
And the loud bittern, from the bull-rush home,
Gave from the salt-ditch side the bellowing boom.
He nursed the feelings these dull scenes produce,
And loved to stop beside the opening sluice;
Where the small stream, confined in narrow bound,
Ran with a dull, unvaried, sadd'ning sound;
Where all presented to the eye or ear
Oppress'd the soul with misery, grief, and fear....

GEORGE CRABBE (1754–1832)

Winter in The Fens

So moping flat and low our valleys lie,
So dull and muggy is our winter sky,
Drizzling from day to day with threats of rain,
And when that falls still threatening on again;
From one wet week so great an ocean flows
That every village to an island grows,
And every road for even weeks to come
Is stopt, and none but horsemen go from home;
And one wet night leaves travel's best in doubt,
And horseback travellers ask if floods are out
Of every passer-by, and with their horse
The meadow's ocean try in vain to cross;
The horse's footings with a sucking sound
Fill up with water on the firmest ground,
And ruts that dribble into brooks elsewhere
Can find no fall or flat to dribble here;
But filled with wet they brim and overflow
Till hollows in the road to rivers grow;
Then wind with sudden rage, abrupt and blea,
Twirls every lingering leaf from off each tree.
Such is our lowland scene that winter gives,
And strangers wonder where our comfort lives;
Yet in a little close, however keen
The winter comes, I find a patch of green,
Where robins, by the miser winter made
Domestic, flirt and perch upon the spade;
And in a little garden-close at home
I watch for spring — and there's the crocus come!

JOHN CLARE (1793–1864)

In hardwood groves

The same leaves over and over again!
They fall from giving shade above,
To make one texture of faded brown
And fit the earth like a leather glove.

Before the leaves can mount again
To fill the trees with another shade,
They must go down past things coming up.
They must go down into the dark decayed.

They *must* be pierced by flowers and put
Beneath the feet of dancing flowers.
However it is in some other world
I know that this is the way in ours.

ROBERT FROST (1875–1963)

The year

The crocus, while the days are dark,
   Unfolds its saffron sheen;
At April's touch, the crudest bark,
   Discovers gems of green.

Then sleep the seasons, full of might;
   While slowly swells the pod
And rounds the peach, and in the night
   The mushroom bursts the sod.

The winter comes: the frozen rut
   Is bound with silver bars;
The snow-drift heaps against the hut;
   And night is pierced with stars.

COVENTRY PATMORE (1823–1896)

Lakeland skating

from: The Prelude

And in the frosty season, when the sun
Was set, and visible for many a mile
The cottage windows blazed through twilight gloom,
I heeded not their summons: happy time
It was indeed for all of us — for me
It was a time of rapture! Clear and loud
The village clock tolled six, — I wheeled about,
Proud and exulting like an untired horse
That cares not for his home. All shod with steel,
We hissed along the polished ice in games
Confederate, imitative of the chase
And woodland pleasures, — the resounding horn,
The pack loud chiming, and the hunted hare.
So through the darkness and the cold we flew,
And not a voice was idle; with the din
Smitten, the precipices rang aloud;
The leafless trees and every icy crag
Tinkled like iron; while far distant hills
Into the tumult sent an alien sound
Of melancholy not unnoticed, while the stars
Eastward were sparkling clear, and in the west
The orange sky of evening died away.
Not seldom from the uproar I retired
Into a silent bay, or sportively
Glanced sideway, leaving the tumultuous throng,
To cut across the reflex of a star
That fled, and, flying still before me, gleamed
Upon the glassy plain; and oftentimes,

When we had given our bodies to the wind,
And all the shadowy banks on either side
Came sweeping through the darkness, spinning still
The rapid line of motion, then at once
Have I, reclining back upon my heels,
Stopped short; yet still the solitary cliffs
Wheeled by me — even as if the earth had rolled
With visible motion her diurnal round!
Behind me did they stretch in solemn train,
Feebler and feebler, and I stood and watched
Till all was tranquil as a dreamless sleep.

WILLIAM WORDSWORTH (1770–1850)

Written in Surrey

My skinny little cherry tree
  alighting without sound
like a feather fallen from
  a cloud to the ground,
you shake, as you shiver there
  bare in the white day
birds out of your nested hair
  and like memories they
grow dark in the evening air
  as they sweep away.
But once above your aery house
  the sun of the blue day
hung among your golden boughs
  and saw the children play
and the summer saunter by
  trailing her hand in the auburn
cornfields of July.
  O skinny little cherry tree
all the memories pass.
  What is the image that you see
shed on the frosty grass?
  Where once on a summer time
lovers and children stood
  an old man without a scythe
gathering up wood.

GEORGE BARKER (1913–   )

Wicken Fen

Nothing is here but sedge-cut skies,
Azure of darting dragon-flies
And horse-flies settling on my flesh
Soft as the touch of spider's mesh.

A plunging pike rocks with a wave
The white-spoked nenuphars that pave
With smooth round leaves the loose-mired lode
That through the fen drives its straight road.

And as the wind blows back the stream
Shaking the buckthorns from their dream,
Time flows back here at Wicken Fen
To swine-steads and blue-woaded men.

Small shaggy men that plunge again
Through sedge and the black rotting rain;
And I too shudder as I feel
The whole earth shake under my heel.

ANDREW YOUNG (1885–1971)

In Romney Marsh

As I went down to Dymchurch Wall,
   I heard the South sing o'er the land;
I saw the yellow sunlight fall
   On knolls where Norman churches stand.

And ringing shrilly, taut and lithe,
   Within the wind a core of sound,
The wire from Romney town to Hythe
   Alone its airy journey wound.

A veil of purple vapour flowed
   And trailed its fringe along the Straits;
The upper air like sapphire glowed;
   And roses filled Heaven's central gates.

Masts in the offing wagged their tops;
   The swinging waves pealed on the shore;
The saffron beach, all diamond drops
   And beads of surge, prolonged the roar.

As I came up from Dymchurch Wall,
   I saw above the Down's low crest
The crimson brands of sunset fall,
   Flicker and fade from out the west.

Night sank: like flakes of silver fire
   The stars in one great shower came down;
Shrill blew the wind; and shrill the wire
   Rang out from Hythe to Romney town.

The darkly shining salt sea drops
   Streamed as the waves clashed on the shore;
The beach, with all its organ stops
   Pealing again, prolonged the roar.

JOHN DAVIDSON (1857-1909)

The ploughman's horse

from: Winter

Sweet then the ploughman's slumbers, hale and young,
When the last topic dies upon his tongue;
Sweet then the bliss his transient dreams inspire,
Till chilblains wake him, or the snapping fire.
He starts, and ever thoughtful of his team,
Along the glittering snow a feeble gleam
Shoots from his lantern, as he yawning goes
To add fresh comforts to their night's repose;
Diffusing fragrance as their food he moves,
And pats the jolly sides of those he loves.
Thus full replenished, perfect ease possessed,
From night till morn alternate food and rest,
No rightful cheer withheld, no sleep debarred,
Their each day's labour brings its sure reward.
Yet when from plough or lumbering cart set free,
They taste awhile the sweets of liberty:
E'en sober Dobbin lifts his clumsy heel
And kicks, disdainful of the dirty wheel;
But soon, his frolic ended, yields again
To trudge the road, and wear the clinking chain.

ROBERT BLOOMFIELD (1766–1823)

Overleaf: Lower Norwood. *Camille Pissarro*

Carmarthenshire landscape

from: Grongar Hill

Now I gain the mountain's brow,
What a landskip lies below!
No clouds, no vapours intervene;
But the gay, the open scene
Does the face of Nature show
In all the hues of heaven's bow,
And, swelling to embrace the light,
Spreads around beneath the sight.
    Old castles on the cliffs arise,
Proudly tow'ring in the skies;
Rushing from the woods, the spires
Seem from hence ascending fires;
Half his beams Apollo sheds
On the yellow mountain-heads,
Gilds the fleeces of the flocks,
And glitters on the broken rocks.
    Below me trees unnumber'd rise,
Beautiful in various dyes;
The gloomy pine, the poplar blue,
The yellow beech, the sable yew,
The slender fir, that taper grows,
The sturdy oak with broad-spread boughs,
And beyond the purple grove,
Haunt of Phillis, queen of love!
Gaudy as the op'ning dawn,
Lies a long and level lawn,
On which a dark hill, steep and high,
Holds and charms the wand'ring eye:
Deep are his feet in Towy's flood,
His sides are cloath'd with waving wood,
And ancient towers crown his brow,
That cast an awful look below;
Whose ragged walls the ivy creeps,
And with her arms from falling keeps;
So both a safety from the wind
On mutual dependence find.

JOHN DYER (1701–1757)

The snowstorm

Announced by all the trumpets of the sky,
Arrives the snow, and, driving o'er the fields,
Seems nowhere to alight: the whited air
Hides hills and woods, the river, and the heaven,
And veils the farmhouse at the garden's end.
The sled and traveller stopped, the courier's feet
Delayed, all friends shut out, the housemates sit
Around the radiant fireplace, enclosed
In a tumultuous privacy of storm.

Come, see the north wind's masonry.
Out of an unseen quarry evermore
Furnished with tile, the fierce artificer
Curves his white bastions with projected roof
Round every windward stake or tree or door.
Speeding, the myriad-handed, his wild work
So fanciful, so savage, naught cares he
For number or proportion. Mockingly
On coop or kennel he hangs Parian wreaths;
A swan-like form invests the hidden thorn;
Fills up the farmer's lane from wall to wall,
Maugre the farmer's sighs; and at the gate
A tapering turret overtops the work.
And when his hours are numbered, and the world
Is all his own, retiring, as he were not.
Leaves, when the sun appears, astonished Art
To mimic in slow structures, stone by stone,
Built in an age, the mad wind's night-work,
The frolic architecture of the snow.

RALPH WALDO EMERSON (1803–1882)

Woods in winter

When winter winds are piercing chill,
  And through the hawthorn blows the gale,
With solemn feet I tread the hill,
  That overbrows the lonely vale.

O'er the bare upland, and away
  Through the long reach of desert woods,
The embracing sunbeams chastely play,
  And gladden these deep solitudes.

Where, twisted round the barren oak,
  The summer vine in beauty clung,
And summer winds the stillness broke,
  The crystal icicle is hung.

Where, from their frozen urns, mute springs
  Pour out the river's gradual tide,
Shrilly the skater's iron rings,
  And voices fill the woodland side.

Alas! how changed from the fair scene,
  When birds sang out their mellow lay,
And winds were soft, and woods were green,
  And the song ceased not with the day!

But still wild music is abroad,
  Pale, desert woods! within your crowd;
And gathering winds, in hoarse accord,
  Amid the vocal reeds pipe loud.

Chill airs and wintry winds! my ear
  Has grown familiar with your song;
I hear it in the opening year,
  I listen, and it cheers me long.

HENRY WADSWORTH LONGFELLOW (1807–1882)

Avenue of Oaks. *J. D. Cooper after W. H. J. Boot*

A frosty day

Grass afield wears silver thatch;
   Palings all are edged with rime;
Frost-flowers pattern round the latch;
   Cloud nor breeze dissolve the clime;

When the waves are solid floor,
   And the clods are iron-bound,
And the boughs are crystall'd hoar,
   And the red leaf nailed a-ground.

When the fieldfare's flight is slow,
   And a rosy vapour rim,
Now the sun is small and low,
   Belts along the region dim.

When the ice-crack flies and flaws,
   Shore to shore, with thunder shock,
Deeper than the evening daws,
   Clearer than the village clock.

When the rusty blackbird strips
   Bunch by bunch, the coral thorn;
And the pale day-crescent dips,
   New to heaven, a slender horn.

LORD DE TABLEY (1835–1895)

Airey-Force Valley

      Not a breath of air
Ruffles the bosom of this leafy glen.
From the brook's margin, wide around, the trees
Are stedfast as the rocks; the brook itself,
Old as the hills that feed it from afar,
Doth rather deepen than disturb the calm
Where all things else are still and motionless.

And yet, even now, a little breeze, perchance
Escaped from boisterous winds that rage without,
Has entered, by the sturdy oaks unfelt,
But to its gentle touch how sensitive
Is the light ash! that, pendent from the brow
Of yon dim cave, in seeming silence makes
A soft eye-music of slow-waving boughs,
Powerful almost as vocal harmony
To stay the wanderer's steps and soothe his thoughts.

WILLIAM WORDSWORTH (1770–1850)

Summer and Winter

It was a bright and cheerful afternoon,
Towards the end of the sunny month of June,
When the north wind congregates in crowds
The floating mountains of the silver clouds
From the horizon — and the stainless sky
Opens beyond them like eternity.
All things rejoiced beneath the sun; the weeds,
The river, and the corn-fields, and the reeds;
The willow leaves that glanced in the light breeze,
And the firm foliage of the larger trees.

It was a winter such as when birds die
In the deep forests; and the fishes lie
Stiffened in the translucent ice, which makes
Even the mud and slime of the warm lakes
A wrinkled clod as hard as brick; and when,
Among their children, comfortable men
Gather about great fires, and yet feel cold:
Alas then for the homeless beggar old!

PERCY BYSSHE SHELLEY (1792–1822)

The Thames

from: Cooper's Hill

The stream is so transparent, pure, and clear,
That had the self-enamour'd youth gaz'd here,
So fatally deceiv'd he had not been,
While he the bottom, not his face had seen.
But his proud head the aery Mountain hides
Among the Clouds; his shoulders, and his sides
A shady mantle cloaths; his curled brows
Frown on the gentle stream, which calmly flows,
While winds and storms his lofty forehead beat:
The common fate of all that's high or great.
Low at his foot a spacious plain is plac't,
Between the mountain and the stream embrac't:
Which shade and shelter from the Hill derives,
While the kind river wealth and beauty gives;
And in the mixture of all these appears
Variety, which all the rest indears.

SIR JOHN DENHAM (1615–1669)

At day-close in November

The ten hours' light is abating,
  And a late bird wings across,
Where the pines, like waltzers waiting,
  Give their black heads a toss.

Beech leaves, that yellow the noon-time,
  Float past like specks in the eye;
I set every tree in my June time,
  And now they obscure the sky.

And the children who ramble through here
  Conceive that there never has been
A time when no tall trees grew here,
  That none will in time be seen.

THOMAS HARDY (1840–1928)

Song

The feathers of the willow
Are half of them grown yellow
  Above the swelling stream;
And ragged are the bushes,
And rusty now the rushes,
  And wild the clouded gleam.

The thistle now is older,
His stalk begins to moulder,
  His head is white as snow;
The branches all are barer,
The linnet's song is rarer,
  The robin pipeth now.

RICHARD WATSON DIXON (1833–1900)   177

The Winter walk at noon

from: The Task

But let the months go round, a few short months,
And all shall be restor'd. These naked shoots,
Barren as lances, among which the wind
Makes wintry music, sighing as it goes,
Shall put their graceful foliage on again,
And, more aspiring, and with ampler spread,
Shall boast new charms, and more than they have lost.
Then, each in its peculiar honours clad,
Shall publish, even to the distant eye,
Its family and tribe. Laburnum, rich
In streaming gold; syringa, iv'ry pure;
The scentless and the scented rose; this red
And of an humbler growth, the other tall,

Driving Sheep. *James Stark*

And throwing up into the darkest gloom
Of neighb'ring cypress, or more sable yew,
Her silver globes, light as the foamy surf
That the wind severs from the broken wave
The lilac, various in array, now white,
Now sanguine, and her beauteous head now set
With purple spikes pyramidal, as if,
Studious of ornament, yet unresolv'd
Which hue she most approv'd, she chose them all;
Copious of flow'rs the woodbine, pale and wan,
But well compensating her sickly looks
With never-cloying odours, early and late;
Hypericum, all bloom, so thick a swarm
Of flow'rs, like flies clothing her slender rods,
That scarce a leaf appears, mezereon, too,
Though leafless, well attir'd, and thick beset
With blushing wreaths, investing ev'ry spray;
Althæa with the purple eye; the broom,
Yellow and bright, as bullion unalloy'd,
Her blossoms; and, luxuriant above all,
The jasmine, throwing wide her elegant sweets,
The deep dark green of whose unvarnish'd leaf
Makes more conspicuous, and illumines more
The bright profusion of her scatter'd stars.—
These have been, and these shall be in their day;
And all this uniform, uncolour'd scene,
Shall be dismantled of its fleecy load,
And flush into variety again.

WILLIAM COWPER (1731–1800)

Forest trees

There stood the elme, whose shade so mildely dym
Doth nourish all that groweth under him:
Cipresse that like piramides runne topping,
And hurt the least of any by their dropping:—
The alder, whose fat shadow nourisheth,
Each plant set neere to him long flourisheth:—
The heavie-headed plane-tree, by whose shade
The grasse grows thickest, men are fresher made:—
The oake, that best endures the thunder-shocks;
The everlasting ebene, cedar, boxe:—
The olive that in wainscot never cleaves:—
The amorous vine which in the elme still weaves:—
The lotus, juniper, where wormes ne'er enter:
The pyne, with whom men through the ocean venter:—
The warlike yewgh, by which (more than the lance,)
The strong-arm'd English spirits conquer'd France:—
Amongst the rest, the tamariske there stood,
For housewives' besomes only knowne most good:—
The cold-place-loving birch, and servis-tree;
The walnut loving vales, and mulberry:—
The maple, ashe, that doe delight in fountaines
Which have their currents by the sides of mountaines:—
The laurell, mirtle, ivy, date, which hold
Their leaves all Winter, be it ne'er so cold:—
The firre, that oftentimes doth rosin drop:
The beech, that seales the welkin with his top:
All these and thousand more within this grove,
By all the industry of nature strove
To frame an arbour that might keepe within it,
The best of beauties that the world hath in it.

WILLIAM BROWNE (1591–1643)

Beech Trees. *Alfred Priest*

Winter's rage

from: The Seasons

With the fierce rage of Winter deep suffus'd,
An icy gale, oft shifting, o'er the pool
Breathes a blue film, and in its mid career
Arrests the bickering stream. The loosened ice,
Let down the flood, and half dissolv'd by day,
Rustles no more; but to the sedgy bank
Fast grows, or gathers round the pointed stone,
A crystal pavement, by the breath of heaven
Cemented firm; till, seiz'd from shore to shore,
The whole imprison'd river growls below.
Loud rings the frozen earth, and hard reflects
A double noise; while, at his evening watch,
The village dog deters the nightly thief;
The heifer lows; the distant waterfall
Swells in the breeze; and, with the hasty tread
Of traveller, the hollow-sounding plain
Shakes from afar. The full ethereal round,
Infinite worlds disclosing to the view,
Shines out intensely keen; and, all one cope
Of starry glitter glows from pole to pole.
  From pole to pole the rigid influence falls,
Through the still night, incessant, heavy, strong,
And seizes Nature fast. It freezes on;
Till morn, late-rising o'er the drooping world,
Lifts her pale eye unjoyous. Then appears
The various labour of the silent night:
Prone from the dripping cave, and dumb cascade,
Whose idle torrents only seem to roar,
The pendant icicle; the frost-work fair,
Where transient hues and fancy'd figures rise;

Wide-spouted o'er the hill the frozen brook,
A livid tract, cold-gleaming on the morn;
The forest bent beneath the plumy wave;
And by the frost refin'd the whiter snow,
Incrusted hard, and sounding to the tread
Of early shepherd, as he pensive seeks
His pining flock, or from the mountain top,
Pleas'd with the slippery surface, swift descends.

JAMES THOMSON (1700–1748)

To Nature

It may indeed be phantasy, when I
    Essay to draw from all created things
    Deep, heartfelt, inward joy that closely clings;
And trace in leaves and flowers that round me lie
Lessons of love and earnest piety.
    So let it be; and if the wide world rings
    In mock of this belief, it brings
Nor fear, nor grief, nor vain perplexity.
So will I build my altar in the fields,
    And the blue sky my fretted dome shall be,
And the sweet fragrance that the wild flower yields
    Shall be the incense I will yield to Thee,
Thee only God! and thou shalt not despise
Even me, the priest of this poor sacrifice.

S. T. COLERIDGE (1772–1834)

The snow

It sifts from leaden sieves,
It powders all the wood,
It fills with alabaster wool
The wrinkles of the road.

It makes an even face
Of mountain and of plain, —
Unbroken forehead from the east
Unto the east again.

It reaches to the fence,
It wraps it, rail by rail,
Till it is lost in fleeces;
It flings a crystal veil

On stump and stack and stem, —
The summer's empty room,
Acres of seams where harvests were,
Recordless, but for them.

It ruffles wrists of posts,
As ankles of a queen, —
Then stills its artisans like ghosts,
Denying they have been.

EMILY DICKINSON (1830–1886)

The Deep Lane. *J. D. Cooper after W. H. J. Boot*

A Field of Green Corn. *William Davis*

Acknowledgments

George Barker, *Written in Surrey*. Reprinted by permission of the author

John Betjeman, *Upper Lambourn* and *Essex*. Reprinted by permission of the author and John Murray (Publishers) Ltd from COLLECTED POEMS by John Betjeman

Edmund Blunden, *Gleaning*. Reprinted by permission of William Collins and Sons from COLLECTED POEMS by Edmund Blunden

Richard Church, *After the storm*. Reprinted by permission of William Heinemann Ltd and the Estate of the late Richard Church from COLLECTED POEMS by Richard Church

Frances Cornford, *The coast: Norfolk* and *Cambridgeshire*. Reprinted by permission of Barrie & Jenkins, and originally published by The Cresset Press

W. H. Davies, *The rain*, *Cowslips and Larks*, and *The woods and banks*. Reprinted by permission of Mrs H. M. Davies and Jonathan Cape Ltd from THE COMPLETE POEMS OF W. H. DAVIES

Robert Frost, *Spring pools* and *In hardwood groves*. Reprinted by permission of the Estate of Robert Frost, Jonathan Cape Ltd and the editor from THE POETRY OF ROBERT FROST (edited by Edward Connery Lathem)

Ivor Gurney, *The Wood of August* and *The Larches*. Reprinted by permission of the author's Literary Estate and Chatto & Windus Ltd from POEMS OF IVOR GURNEY 1890–1937

Seamus Heaney, *The peninsula*. Reprinted by permission of Faber and Faber Ltd from DOOR INTO THE DARK by Seamus Heaney

Ted Hughes, *March morning unlike others* and *The Harvest Moon*. Reprinted by permission of Faber and Faber Ltd, from SEASON SONGS by Ted Hughes

Rudyard Kipling, *Sussex 1902*. Reprinted by permission of The National Trust and Eyre Methuen & Co Ltd

Philip Larkin, *The trees*. Reprinted by permission of Faber and Faber Ltd from HIGH WINDOWS by Philip Larkin

Louis MacNeice, *Under the mountains*. Reprinted by permission of Faber and Faber Ltd from THE COLLECTED POEMS OF LOUIS MACNEICE

John Masefield, *Up on the downs*. Reprinted by permission of the Society of Authors as the literary representative of the Estate of John Masefield

Norman Nicholson, *The oak tree*. Reprinted by permission of Faber and Faber Ltd from THE POT GERANIUM by Norman Nicholson

W. R. Rodgers, *The harvest field*. Reprinted by permission of Martin Secker & Warburg Ltd from EUROPA AND THE BULL by W. R. Rodgers

V. Sackville-West, *The Weald of Kent*. Reprinted by permission of Nigel Nicolson from THE LAND

Vernon Watkins, *Cornfields*. Reprinted by permission of Mrs G. Watkins from FIDELITIES by Vernon Watkins (Faber and Faber Ltd, 1968)

W. B. Yeats, 'I walked among the seven woods of Coole' from *The shadowy waters*. Reprinted by permission of M. B. Yeats, Miss Anne Yeats and the Macmillan Company of London and Basingstoke

Andrew Young, *Wicken Fen* and *Stay, Spring*. Reprinted by permission of Martin Secker and Warburg Ltd from COMPLETE POEMS by Andrew Young

Index to Authors

Akenside, Mark, 54
Arnold, Matthew, 83, 106

Barker, George, 164
Barnes, William, 29, 78
Barton, Bernard, 71
Betjeman, John, 52, 100
Bloomfield, Robert, 87, 167
Blunden, Edmund, 141
Brontë, Charlotte, 83
Brooke, Rupert, 86
Browne, William, 80, 180
Browning, Robert, 38
Burns, Robert, 26

Carew, Thomas, 42
Church, Richard, 19
Clare, John, 75, 101, 114, 138, 160
Clough, Arthur Hugh, 151
Coleridge, Hartley, 151
Coleridge, S. T., 134, 183
Cornford, Frances, 95, 129
Cornish, William, 23
Cowper, William, 81, 178
Crabbe, George, 103, 159

Darwin, Erasmus, 66
Davidson, John, 166
Davies, W. H., 28, 34, 94
Denham, Sir John, 176
Dickinson, Emily, 58, 123, 184
Dixon, Richard Watson, 155, 177
Doubleday, Thomas, 79
Drayton, Michael, 104
Dryden, John, 13
Dyer, John, 73, 170

Ellison, Henry, 124
Emerson, Ralph Waldo, 171

Frost, Robert, 31, 161

Goldsmith, Oliver, 102
Gray, Thomas, 133
Gurney, Ivor, 73, 94

Hardy, Thomas, 18, 153, 177
Heaney, Seamus, 74
Herrick, Robert, 91, 117
Hogg, James, 128
Hopkins, Gerard Manley, 152
Hughes, Ted, 35, 107

Jenner, Charles, 90

Keats, John, 22, 106
King, Henry, 96
Kipling, Rudyard, 110

Larkin, Philip, 43
Longfellow, Henry Wadsworth, 172

MacNeice, Louis, 154
Masefield, John, 39
Meredith, George, 129, 132, 149
Milton, John, 61, 65
Morris, William, 99, 158

Nash, Thomas, 105
Nicholson, Norman, 126

Palmer, Samuel, 136
Patmore, Coventry, 36, 161
Pope, Alexander, 34

Rodgers, W. R., 140
Rossetti, Christina, 44, 69

Sackville-West, V., 84
Shakespeare, William, 102, 139
Shelley, Percy Bysshe, 95, 145, 175
Smart, Christopher, 56
Solomon, Song of, 15

Tabley, Lord De, 174

Tannahill, Robert, 82
Tennyson, Alfred, Lord, 32, 48
Thomas, Edward, 23, 122, 158
Thomson, James, 20, 47, 55, 121, 182

Warton, Thomas, 30
Watkins, Vernon, 62

White, Gilbert, 70
Whitman, Walt, 103
Wordsworth, William, 17, 50, 92, 108, 162, 174

Yeats, W. B., 49
Young, Andrew, 27, 165

Index to Artists

Abbott, John White, 135

Bevan, Robert, 37
Bewick, Thomas, 8, 11, 15, 54, 59, 119, 126, 147, 163, 188
Bowler, H. A., 33
Brown, Ford Madox, 98
Burchett, Richard, 115

Collier, Thomas, 40 & 41
Collinson, Robert, 144
Constable, John, 24 & 25
Constable, Lionel, 116
Cooper, James D. (after W. H. J. Boot), 173, 185
Cotman, J. S., front endpaper
Cotman, Miles Edmund, 125
Crome, John, 43, 77

Davis, William, 186

Finden, Edward (after William Westall), 108
Fisher, Mark, 46
Foster, Birket, 64

Gainsborough, Thomas, 63, 88 & 89
Gilman, Harold, 72
Gore, Spencer, 105

Hearne, Thomas, 150

Inchbold, J. W., 45

Lewis, G. R., 143
Linnell, John, 130 & 131, 139
Lucas, David (after John Constable), 101

Middleton, John, 28
Millais, J. E., 85
Mote, George William, 13

Palmer, Samuel, 93, 113, 137, 156 & 157
Pissarro, Camille, 168 & 169
Priest, Alfred, 181

Redgrave, Richard, 66 & 67

Spencer, Stanley, 97
Stark, James, 178
Sutherland, Graham, 68

Taylor, W. (after T. Allom), frontispiece
Towne, Francis, 21
Turner, J. M. W., 51

Watts, G. F., 18
Wilson, Richard, 176
Wint, Peter De, back endpaper